Dedication

Dear Amma and Appa, who ingrained my DNA (Do Not Assume); Dear Padma Athai, who rapped me on me knuckles every time I got punctuation, grammar or spelling wrong.

And

Dearest Revu, *au revoir*

Prologue

"It is Modi's guarantee that India will be among the top three economies in the world in the next 5 years."
PM in his 77th Independence Day Speech

"My dear, here we must run as fast as we can, just to stay in place. And if you wish to go anywhere you must run twice as fast as that. "
― Lewis Carroll, Alice in Wonderland
(The Red Queen Effect)

Top 5 largest economies in the world in 2023

IMF World Economic Outlook 2023 GDP, Current Prices

Rank & Country	GDP (USD billion)
#1 USA	26.85 thousand
#2 China	19.37 thousand
#3 Germany	4.31 thousand
#4 India	3.74 thousand
#5 United Kingdom	3.16 thousand

IMF World Economic Outlook 2023 GDP, Current Prices, PPP

Rank & Country	GDP (USD billion)
#1 China	33.01 thousand
#2 USA	26.85 thousand
#3 India	13.03 thousand
#4 Germany	5.55 thousand
#5 France	3.87 thousand

Even as the PM was addressing the nation on its 77th Independence Day, the nation had already become the third largest economy, measuring GDP in international dollars (Purchasing Power Parity.)

Preface

"Thani oru manithanukku unavillai ennil, Jagathinai azhithiduvom…"

Mahakavi Subramania Bharati

(If a single person does not have food we will destroy this world.)

The trigger for this booklet is multipronged. India's population surpassing China; India becoming the world's third largest economy measuring GDP in international dollars (Purchasing Power Parity.); India Makes First Landing in Moon's Southern Polar Region; India, according to the Global Hunger Index 2022, falls under the Serious 20.0 – 34.9 Category; the World Happiness Report 2023 ranking the happiest countries in the world gave the top spot to Finland for the sixth year in a row; India's G20 Presidency and hosting of the 2023 Summit; India conducted its last decennial census in 2011;

I looked for clues in The DataBank of the World Bank, a benevolence. I have strived to remain objective. This compilation is the result.

Introduction

"Unless we act now, the 2030 Agenda will become an epitaph for a world that might have been."
— António GUTERRES
Secretary-General of the United Nations

This doesn't pretend to be a book on Political Economics. It is a compilation, pure and simple, of indicators relating to India, from the
World Bank's DataBank, focusing on WDI (World Development Indicators) (WDI) and its playbook, World Economic Forum (WEF), IMF (International Monetary Fund), and several other global index builders.

I confess to piggybacking on those giant intellects whose mission is to impoverish poverty, and attain the 17 Sustainable Development Goals (SDG).

The Sustainable Development Goals Report 2023: Special Edition has been released.

While India has become the third largest economy (GDP, PPP), it is ranked at 112(SDG score: 63.45) behind Bangladesh ranked at 101 (SDGscore: 65.91) - https://dashboards.sdgindex.org/rankings.

The 2023 SDG Summit will take place on 18-19 September 2023 in New York. It will mark the beginning of a new phase of accelerated progress towards the Sustainable Development Goals with high-level political guidance on transformative and accelerated actions leading up to 2030.

Convened by the President of the General Assembly, the Summit will mark the half-way point to the deadline set for achieving the 2030 Agenda and the Sustainable Development Goals. It will be the centerpiece of the High-level Week of the General Assembly. It will respond to the impact of multiple and interlocking crises facing the world and is expected to reignite a sense of hope, optimism, and enthusiasm for the 2030 Agenda.

The midway performance of SDG 2030 is briefly reviewed in the latter part of this compilation. It is a wake up call, especially for India.

India' s sight is fixed on 2024 right now. Be that as it may be, India' s mantra ought to be:

The author gratefully acknowledges the generous support, access to the DataBank and WDI. and the implicit permission to use the data and charts.

This exercise would' ve achieved its purpose if one poor person were to cross the global poverty line.

May the world become a better place for everyone.

World Bank Group Country Classifications by Income FY24

The World Bank Group assigns the world's economies to four income groups –
low, lower-middle, upper-middle, and high. The classifications are updated each
year on July 1, based on the GNI per capita of the previous calendar year. GNI
measures are expressed in United States dollars using conversion factors derived
according to the Atlas method, which in its current form was introduced in 1989.
The World Bank's income classification aims to reflect a country's level of
development, drawing on Atlas GNI per capita as a broadly available indicator of
economic capacity.

The World Bank's official estimates of the size of economies and country
classifications by income level are based on Gross National Income (GNI) per
capita. For cross-national comparisons, estimates are converted from local
currency units (LCU) to current U.S. dollars using the Atlas method, referring to a
former World Bank publication called the Atlas of Global Development. The Atlas
method smooths exchange rate fluctuations using a three-year moving average,
price-adjusted conversion factor.

(https://blogs.worldbank.org/opendata/new-world-bank-group-country-
classifications-income-level-fy24#comment-582815)

**India moved from Low Income Group in 2006 to Lower Middle Income Group in
2007 (Interactive map) and continues to remain there now.**

(This map adorns the book's jacket.)

Not surprisingly, of countries changing income categories in 2022, virtually all
moved to a higher category as the recovery from the COVID-19 pandemic
continued. In terms of Atlas GNI per capita, roughly 80% of countries showed
improvement in 2022 *vis-à-vis* the pre-pandemic period (2019).

El Salvador, Indonesia, and West Bank and Gaza all had Atlas GNI very close to
the upper-middle income threshold in 2021, so modest GDP growth in 2022 was
enough to bring these economies into this category.

Five Institutions, One Group

The World Bank Group consists of five organizations:

The International Bank for Reconstruction and Development

The International Bank for Reconstruction and Development (IBRD) lends to governments of middle-income and creditworthy low-income countries.

The International Development Association

The International Development Association (IDA) provides interest-free loans — called credits — and grants to governments of the poorest countries.

Together, IBRD and IDA make up the World Bank.

The International Finance Corporation

The International Finance Corporation (IFC) is the largest global development institution focused exclusively on the private sector. We help developing countries achieve sustainable growth by financing investment, mobilizing capital in international financial markets, and providing advisory services to businesses and governments.

The Multilateral Investment Guarantee Agency

The Multilateral Investment Guarantee Agency (MIGA) was created in 1988 to promote foreign direct investment into developing countries to support economic growth, reduce poverty, and improve people's lives. MIGA fulfills this mandate by offering political risk insurance (guarantees) to investors and lenders.

The International Centre for Settlement of Investment Disputes

The International Centre for Settlement of Investment Disputes (ICSID) provides international facilities for conciliation and arbitration of investment disputes.

"The World Development Indicators is the World Bank′s premier compilation of cross-country comparable data on development. The database currently includes around 1,600 time-series indicators for almost 220 economies and more than 45 country groups, with data for many indicators going back more than 50 years."

Our Mission
The World Bank has two goals: end extreme poverty and promote shared prosperity in a sustainable way.

2022 GLOBAL HUNGER INDEX BY SEVERITY

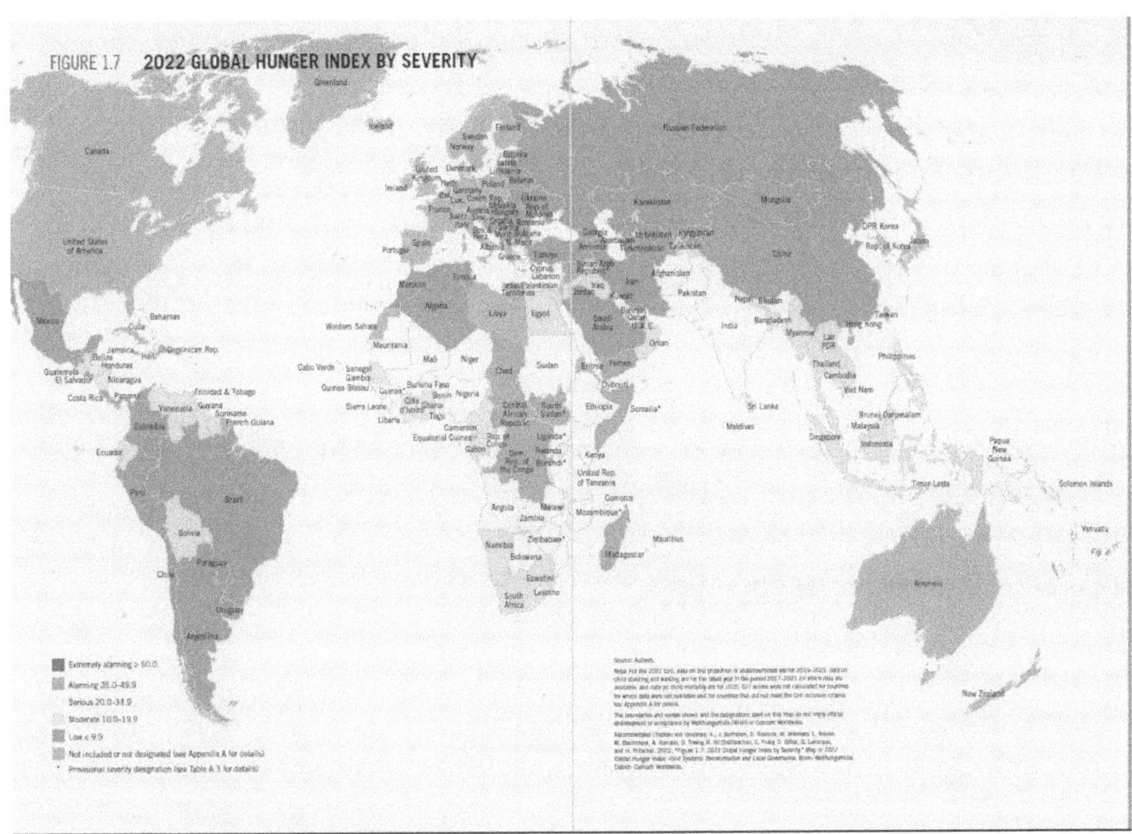

India falls under Serious 20.0–34.9 Category.

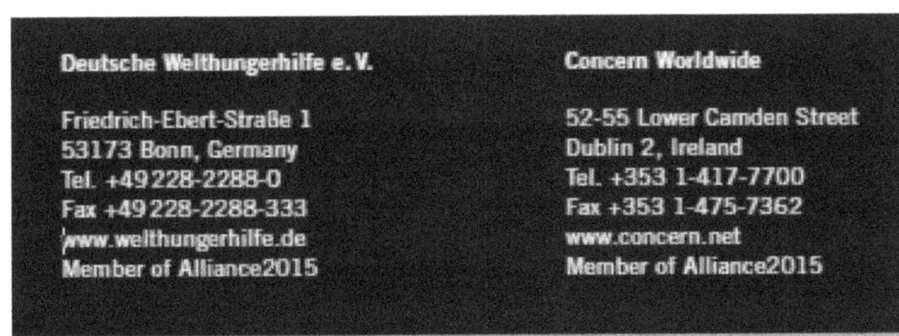

Learning Poverty

Eliminating learning poverty, defined as the share of children that by age 10 cannot read and understand a simple text, is as critical as eliminating extreme poverty, stunting or hunger. Societies, parents, and students know this, and have extraordinary faith in the power of education to transform lives. However, these benefits depend on the actual skills that students acquire. Families invest in education and send their kids to school, but years spent at school don't matter if they are not reflected in learning.

The analysis of the impact of education in future earnings supports this, showing that quality of education matters more than years of schooling. Adults who finish primary with no learning earn only 6% more than those with no schooling, while those that finish primary and learn to read earn 38% more than those with no schooling (Wodon et al., forthcoming).

Learning poverty is today at 53 percent in low- and middle-income countries. So, for children who are not able to read, concerted and dramatic action is needed to help them catch-up. If not, education's promise will be a mere fantasy to them.

The DataBank

The DataBank provides access to 85 Databases, 266 countries/economies, 1478 series and 63 time periods and lets the researcher select the variables, and create a Time Function.

For the purpose of demo, the WDI Database, India, Population Density (people per sq. km of land area) and People practicing open defecation (% of population), the period 2004 - 2022 using Exponential growth rate were selected.

It also offers a selection of data presentation from the tabs Table, Chart, and Map, and three download options - Excel, CSV and Tabbed TXT and Advanced options.

WDI is the primary World Bank collection of development indicators, compiled from officially-recognized international sources. It presents the most current and accurate global development data available, and includes national, regional and global estimates.

Below is a snip of the chart obtained. (Please click and magnify.)

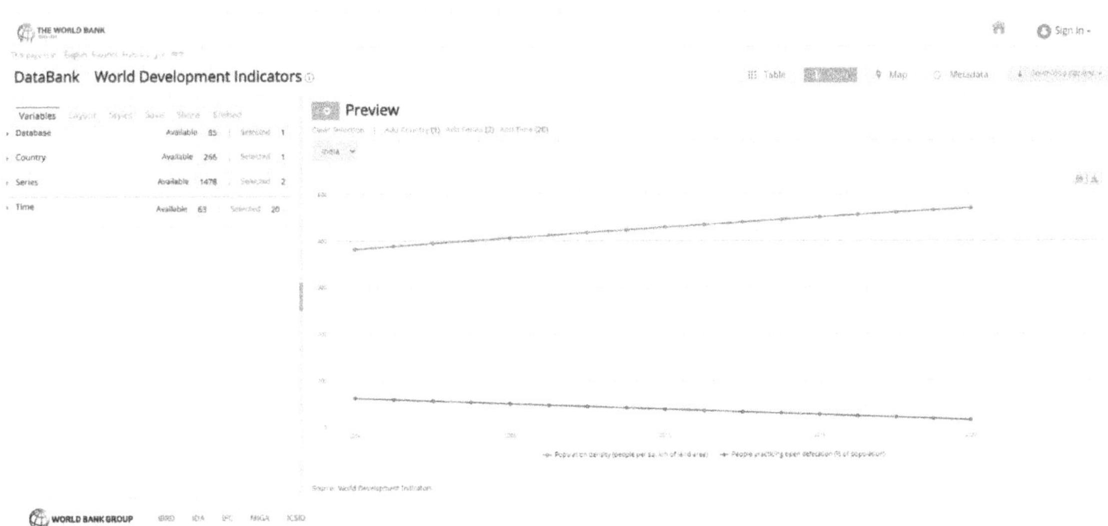

India Meta Data

https://databank.worldbank.org/views/reports/reportwidget.aspx?Report_Name=CountryProfile&Id=b450fd57&tbar=y&dd=y&inf=n&zm=n&country=IND

Statistical Performance Indicators

National statistical systems are facing significant challenges. These challenges arise from increasing demands for high quality and trustworthy data to guide decision making, coupled with the rapidly changing landscape of the data revolution. To help create a mechanism for learning amongst national statistical systems, the World Bank has developed improved Statistical Performance Indicators (SPI) to monitor the statistical performance of countries. The SPI focuses on five key dimensions of a country's statistical performance: (i) data use, (ii) data services, (iii) data products, (iv) data sources, and (v) data infrastructure. (This will replace the Statistical Capacity Index (SCI) that the World Bank has regularly published since 2004.)

The SPI are composed of more than 50 indicators and contain data for 174 countries. This set of countries covers 99.2 percent of the world population. The data extend from 2016-2019, with some indicators going back to 2004.

GDP ranking - Gross domestic product ranking table.

GDP ranking, PPP based - Gross domestic product ranking table based on purchasing power parity (PPP)

Side bar

Purchasing-power parity (PPP)

A method of adjusting exchange rates to take account of the different levels of prices in different countries. In the absence of barriers to trade, theory suggests that the prices of goods and services in different countries should be roughly equivalent (allowing for transport costs). In practice, this is rarely the case. But economists calculate PPP exchange rates as a way of assessing whether currencies are under- or over-valued;

The Economist does this in a light-hearted way with its Big Mac index, which uses the prices of McDonald's burgers.

https://www.economist.com/economics-a-to-z

Implied PPP conversion rate

National currency per international dollar

The higher the factor, the better. The factor for India in 2023 is 23.41

For measuring overall well-being, Purchasing Power Parity (PPP) is considered a good indicator.

China has the highest GDP (PPP). India is at # 3.

(https://www.imf.org/external/datamapper/PPPEX@WEO/OEMDC)

Side bar:

Gross Domestic Product (GDP) from Night Lights [2010]

Nighttime lights satellite imagery and the LandScan population grid provide an alternative means for measuring economic activity. This data is based on a scientific model for creating a disaggregated map of estimated total (formal plus informal) economic activity for countries and states of the world. Regression models were developed to calibrate the sum of lights to official measures of economic activity at the sub-national level for China, India, Mexico, and the United States and at the national level for other countries of the world, and subsequently unique coefficients were derived. Multiplying the unique coefficients with the sum of lights provided estimates of total economic activity, which were spatially distributed to generate a spatially disaggregated 1 km^2 map of total economic activity.

(The vintage date of this data set is 2010.)

UNPD uses total income, whereas the World Bank uses per capita income to measure development.

Reality Check

Hurrah! India has won the GDP PPP Bronze.

How does that translate at the individual citizen level?

The IMF computes this measure to assess that:

GDP per capita, current prices
Purchasing power parity; international dollars per capita

An interactive map tracks the GDP per capita trend from 1980-2028.

https://www.imf.org/external/datamapper/PPPPC@WEO/OEMDC/ADVEC/WEOWORLD/CHN/USA/IND?year=2023

India transitioned from the lowest group (under 1,000) to the 1,000-5,000 group in 1989; and from there to the 5,000-15,000 group in 2013; and continues to linger there.

Below is a snapshot of the map for the year 2023:

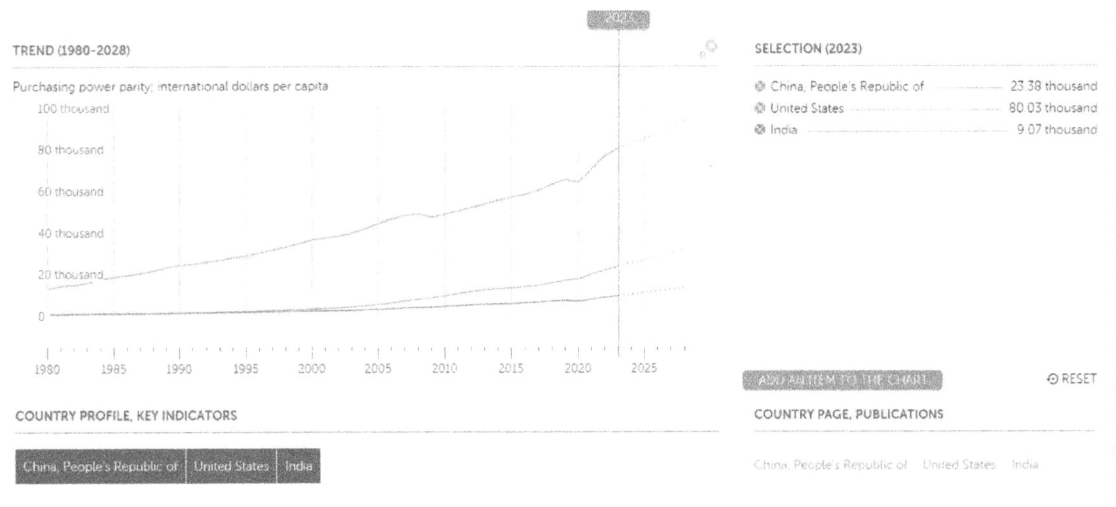

India is ranked 127 out of 192 countries on GDP per capita PPP

https://en.wikipedia.org/wiki/List_of_countries_by_GDP_(PPP)_per_capita

India Trend Line

A comparison of GDP per capita performance under two regimes

2004-2014 and 2014-2024

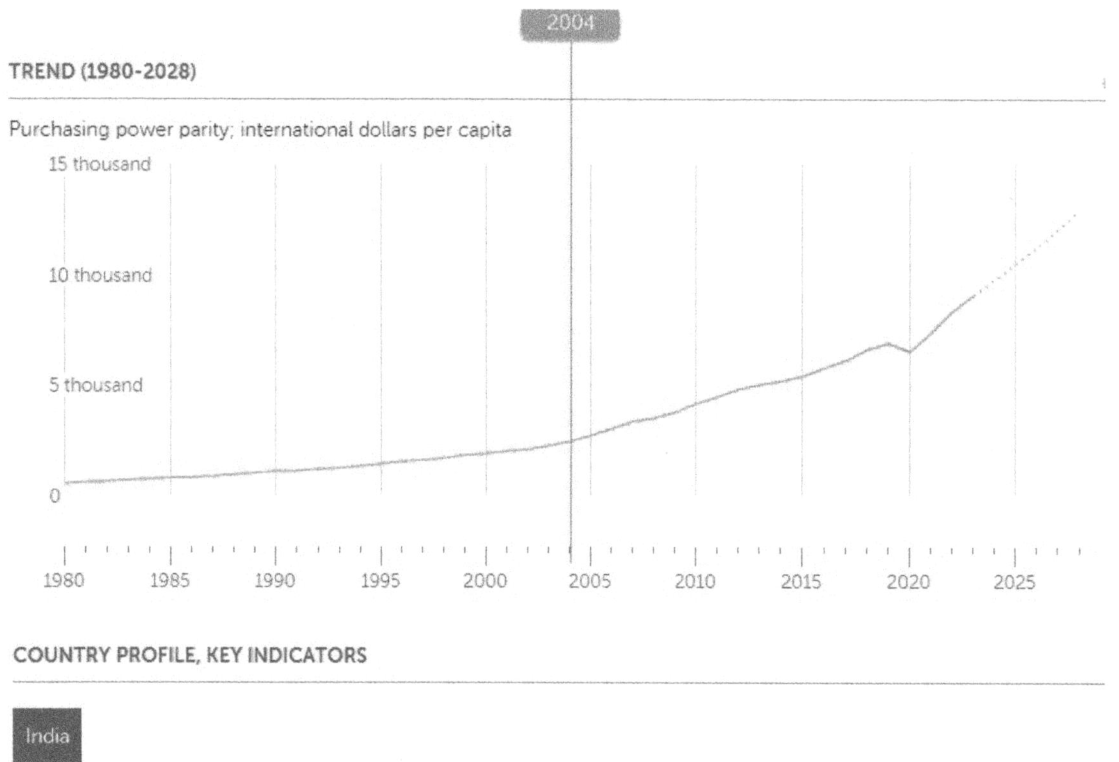

Grew from 2.46 thousand in 2004 to 5.19 thousand in 2014, an increase of 110.98%; from 5.19 thousand in 2014 to 9.77 thousand in 2024 (projected,) an increase of 88.25%.

Indonesia has a GDP per capita of $11,400 as of 2020, while in India, the GDP per capita is $6,100 as of 2020. In Indonesia, 5.3% of adults are unemployed as of 2018. In India, that number is 8.5% as of 2017. In Indonesia, 9.4% live below the poverty line as of 2019.

Some key WDI groups are listed below:

Statistical Capacity Indicators (Public)

Statistical Capacity Indicators provides information on various aspects of national statistical systems of developing countries, including an overall country-level statistical capacity indicator.

Education Statistics - All Indicators (Public)

The World Bank EdStats Query holds around 2,500 internationally comparable education indicators for access, progression, completion, literacy, teachers, population, and expenditures. The indicators cover the education cycle from pre-primary to tertiary education. The query also holds learning outcome data from international learning assessments (PISA, TIMSS, etc.), equity data from household surveys, and projection data to 2050.

Gender Statistics (Public)

Data on key gender topics. Themes included are demographics, education, health, labor force, and political participation.

Health Nutrition and Population Statistics (Public)

Key health, nutrition and population statistics gathered from a variety of international sources.

Millennium Development Goals (Public)

Database of official indicators for monitoring progress toward Millennium Development Goals.

User Guide to WDI Resources

https://datatopics.worldbank.org/world-development-indicators/user-guide.html

Top 25 most popular WDI indicators

GDP (current US$)

Population, total

GDP growth (annual %)

GDP per capita (current US$)

GINI index (World Bank estimate)

Population, female (% of total)

Fertility rate, total (births per woman)

GDP per capita, PPP (current international $)

Life expectancy at birth, total (years)

Military expenditure (% of GDP)

Inflation, consumer prices (annual %)

population (% of total)

Population density (people per sq. km of land area)

CO2 emissions (metric tons per capita)

Health expenditure, total (% of GDP)

Population growth (annual %)

International tourism, number of arrivals

GDP per capita growth (annual %)

Foreign direct investment, net inflows (BoP, current US$)

Government expenditure on education, total (% of GDP)

Literacy rate, adult total (% of people ages 15 and above)

Access to electricity (% of population)

Unemployment, total (% of total labor force) (modeled ILO estimate)

Exports of goods and services (% of GDP)

Mortality rate, infant (per 1,000 live births)

These are examined in the pages that follow.

Poverty Indicators

'Please, sir, I want some more.'

Oliver Twist
Charles Dickens

The world has experienced substantial but uneven progress in poverty reduction over the past three decades. The world has seen significant transformations in its demographic and economic structures in recent times. In 2022, the world's population surpassed 8 billion for the first time and, this year, India (a lower-middle-income country) has overtaken China (an upper-middle-income country) as the world's most populous country.

Absolute poverty captures deprivations in basic needs, such as food, clothing, and shelter, and absolute measures of poverty are fixed in real terms across time and space. Relative poverty accounts for the lack of resources to participate adequately in one's society as it progresses. Measures of relative poverty are defined in relation to a typical measure of economic well-being (e.g., having a disposable income less than 60% of the median in the OECD). Beyond the satisfaction of basic needs, an individual would still feel poor if they are unable to afford a decent lifestyle expected of them in the society in which they live. Relative poverty, therefore, also captures inequality. More recently, societal poverty has been conceptualized as a middle ground for defining poverty, capturing both absolute and relative notions of poverty.

The World Bank has official poverty lines that reflect these different concepts of poverty. These include $2.15, $3.65, $6.85, and max($2.15, $1.15 + 50% of median consumption or income), all expressed in 2017 PPP (more details on these lines below). The first three lines are the absolute poverty lines typical of low-, lower-middle-, and upper-middle-income countries, respectively.3 As the income status of a country increases, so does its national poverty line, reflecting the relative concept of poverty. The societal poverty line incorporates both absolute and relative concepts of poverty.

The international poverty line, currently set at $2.15, is the standard metric for monitoring extreme poverty in the world. This standard is based on the poverty lines used in the poorest countries of the world, which are often set to reflect the budget necessary to afford enough food to meet basic daily caloric needs. If an individual lives on less than $2.15 a day, they are counted as living in extreme poverty.

https://datatopics.worldbank.org/world-development-indicators/stories/where-do-the-poor-live.html

Diet Costs

Cost of a healthy diet in India in 2021: $3.07 ($2.17 is the poverty threshold.)

Number of people who cannot afford a healthy diet in 2021: 1043 million (74.1% of the population)

Affordability is expressed as the diet cost as a percentage of the food component of the international poverty line defined as 52 percent of $1.90 per day in 2011 prices, and equal to $0.99 in 2011 prices.

Ratio of the cost of a healthy diet to the food poverty line component of the international poverty line, 2017 to 2021: 2.66 to 1 (2020)

A healthy diet is considered not affordable when the cost exceeds 52 percent of household income. The cost of a healthy diet is the cost of purchasing the least expensive locally available foods to meet requirements for energy and food-based dietary guidelines in current PPP$/person/day, for a representative person within energy balance at 2330 kcal/day.

https://www.worldbank.org/en/programs/icp/brief/foodpricesfornutrition

By SDG Goal

SDGs,SPIs and WDIs (World Development Indicators)

Statistical Performance Indicators:

The SPI framework focuses on five key pillars of a country's statistical performance: (i) data use, (ii) data services, (iii) data products, (iv) data sources, and (v) data infrastructure. The SPI will replace the Statistical Capacity Indicator (SCI) that the World Bank has regularly published since 2004.

The SPI are composed of more than 50 indicators and contain data for 174 countries. This set of countries covers 99.2 percent of the world population. The data extend from 2016-2019, with some indicators going back to 2004.

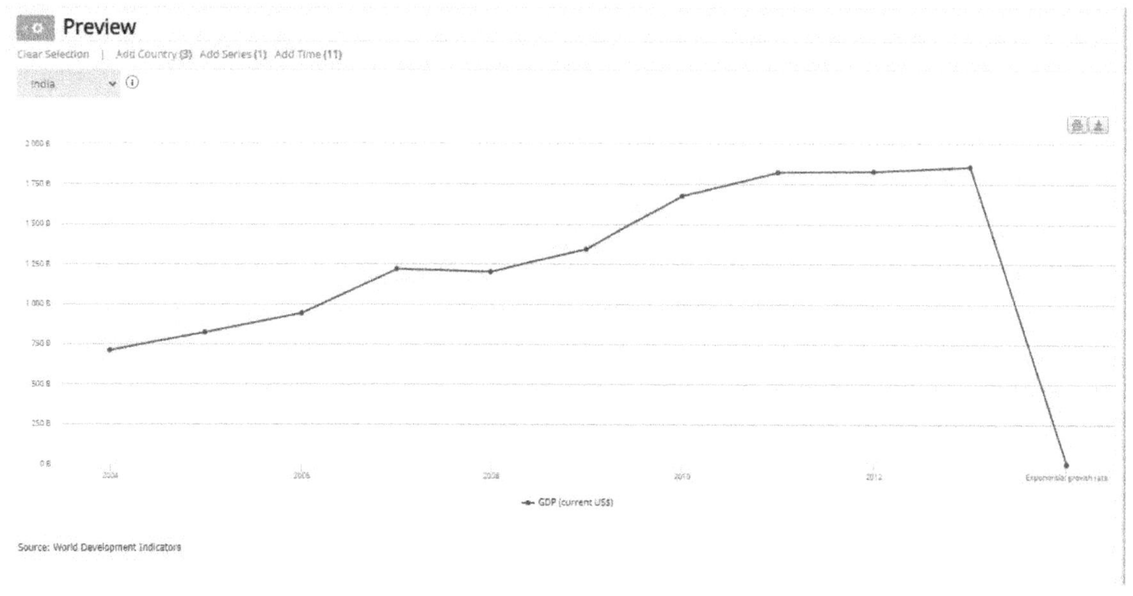

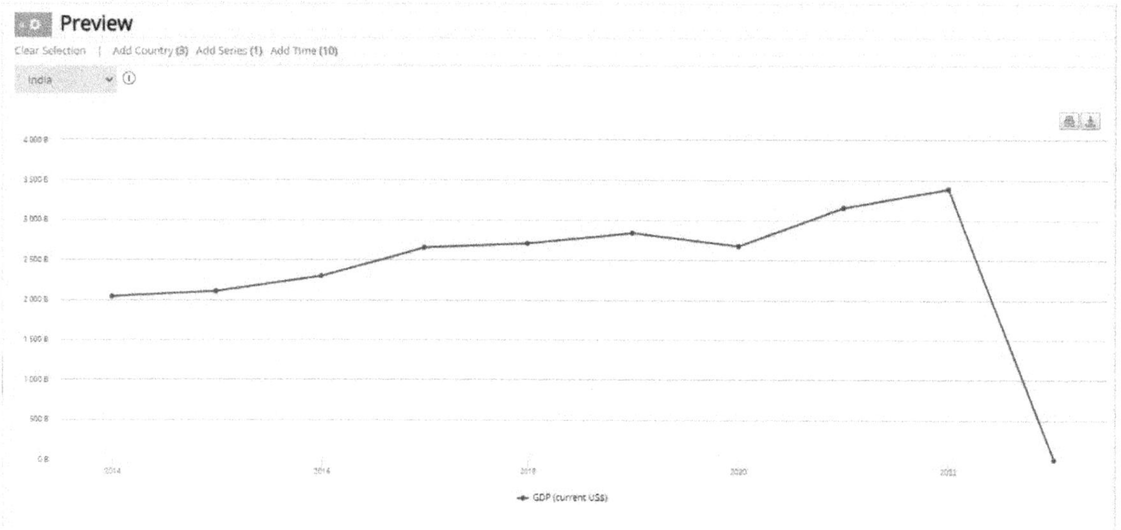

Period	Exponential Growth Rate	Number of Years
2004-2013	11.17	10
2014-2022	6.34	9

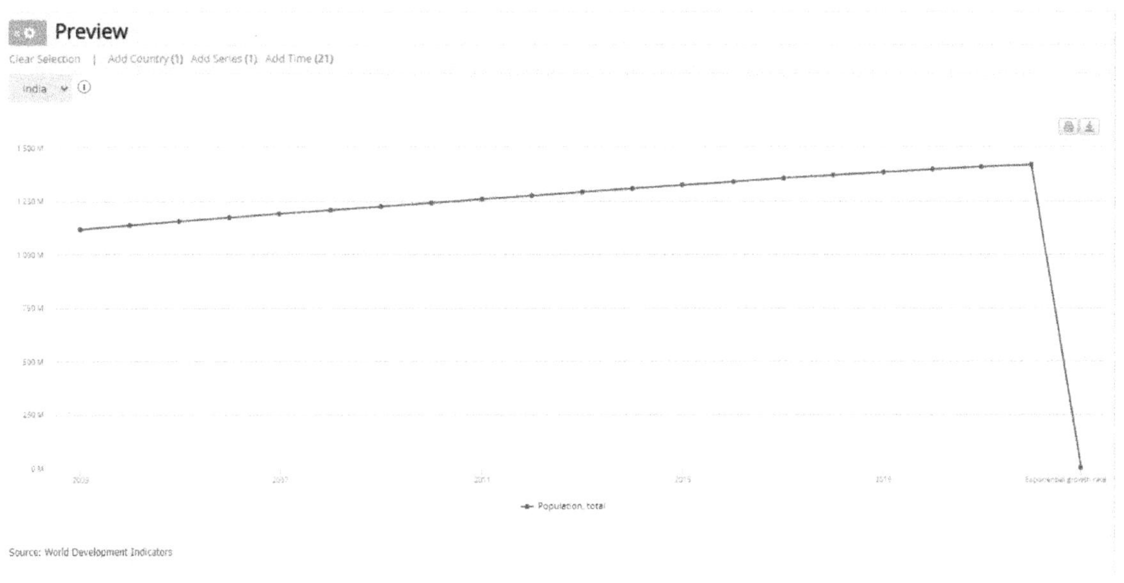

Exponential growth rate: 1.25

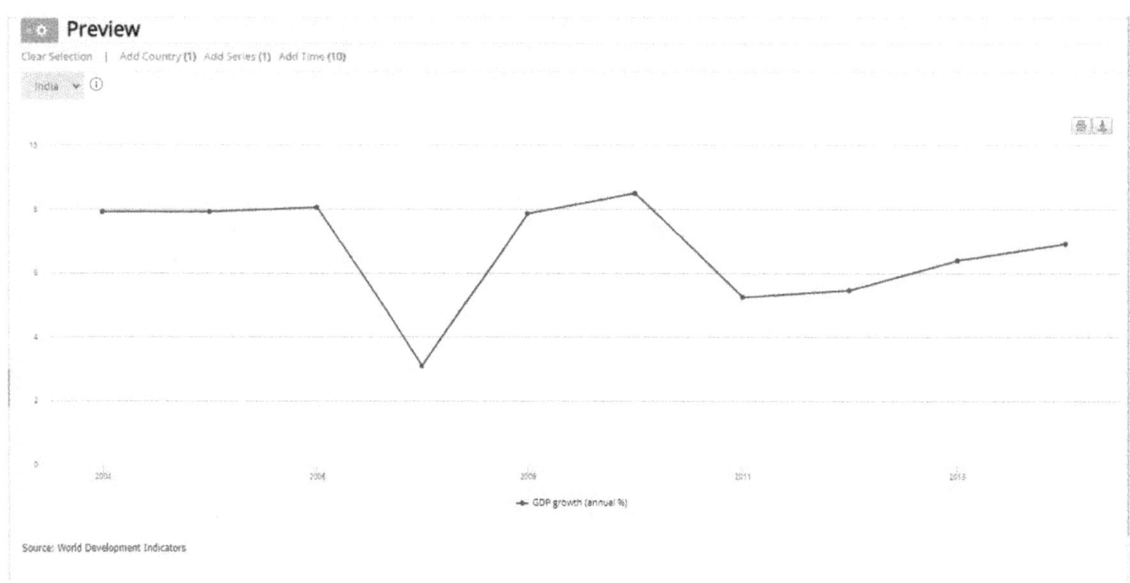

2004-2013 Average GDP growth rate: 6.91

2008 Meltdown

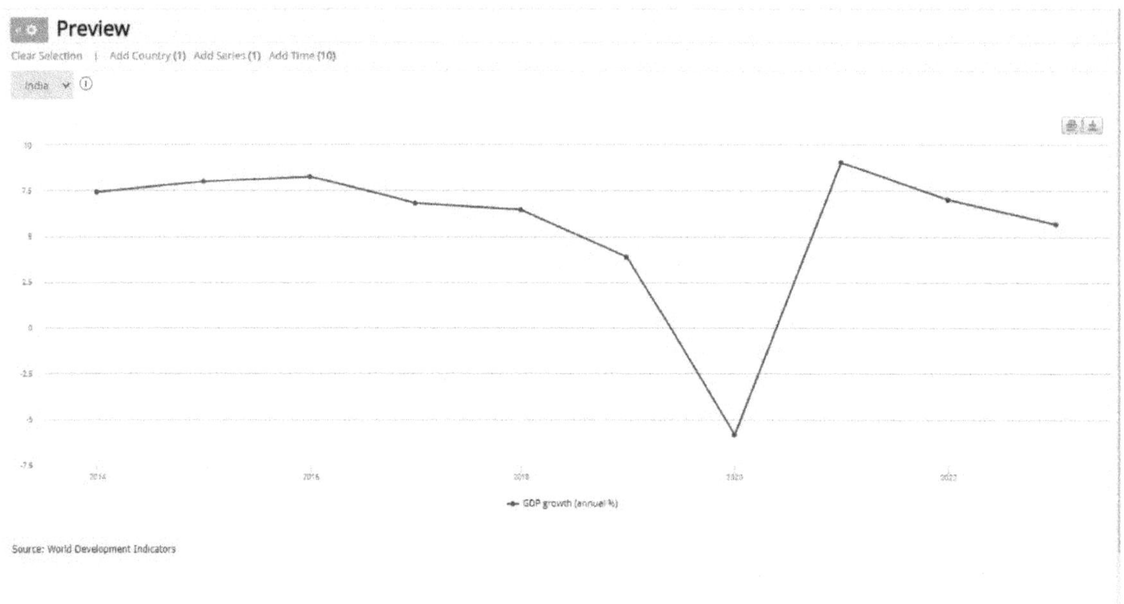

2014-2022 Average GDP growth rate 5.67

2020 - COVID 19

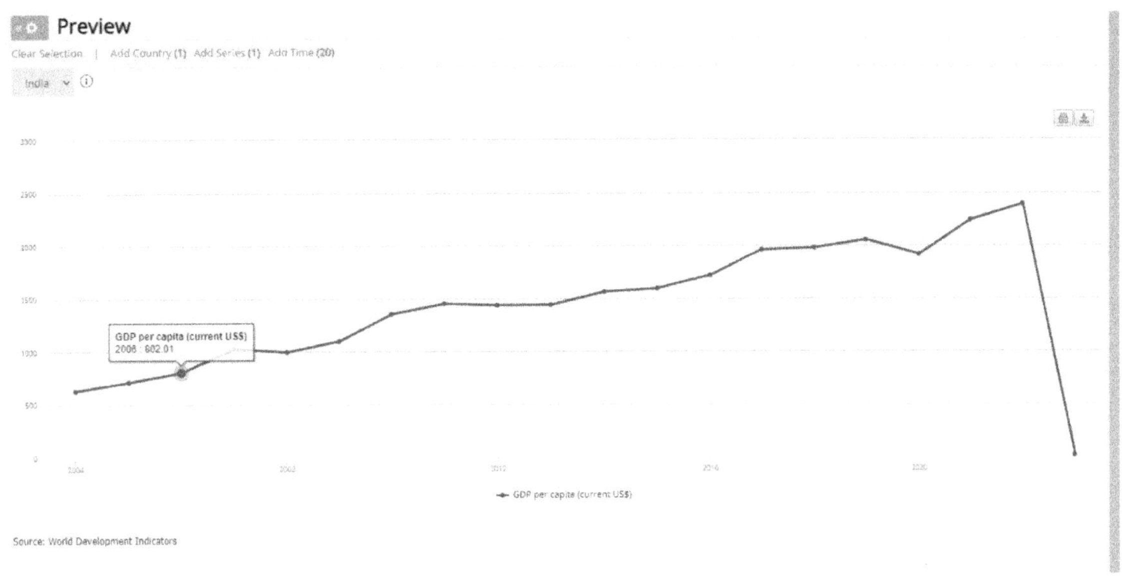

2013-2022 GDP per capita (current US$) growth rate: **7.46**

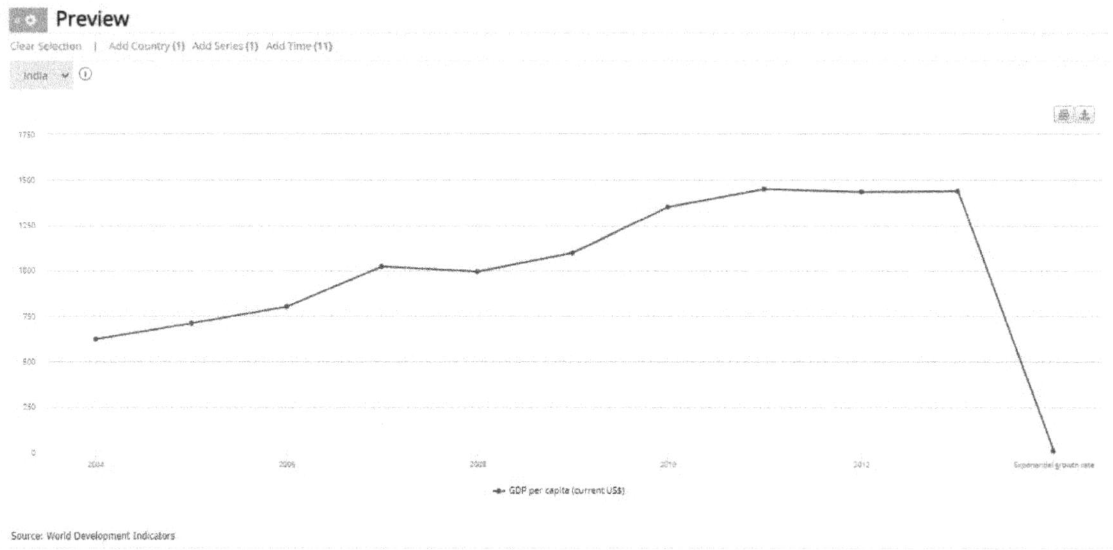

2004-2013 GDP per capita growth (current US$) **9.27**

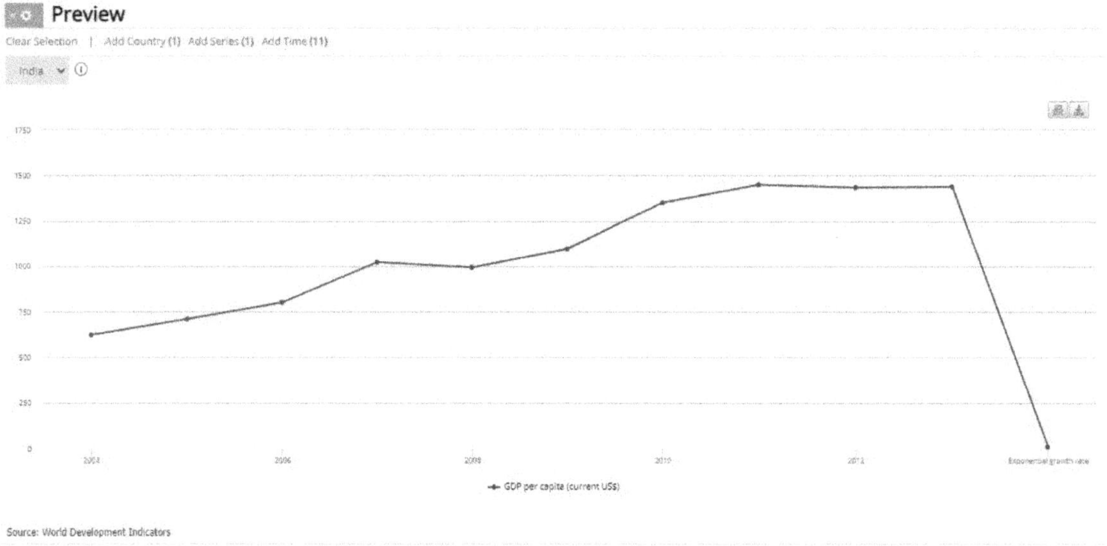

2014-2022 GDP per capita growth (current US$) **5.33**

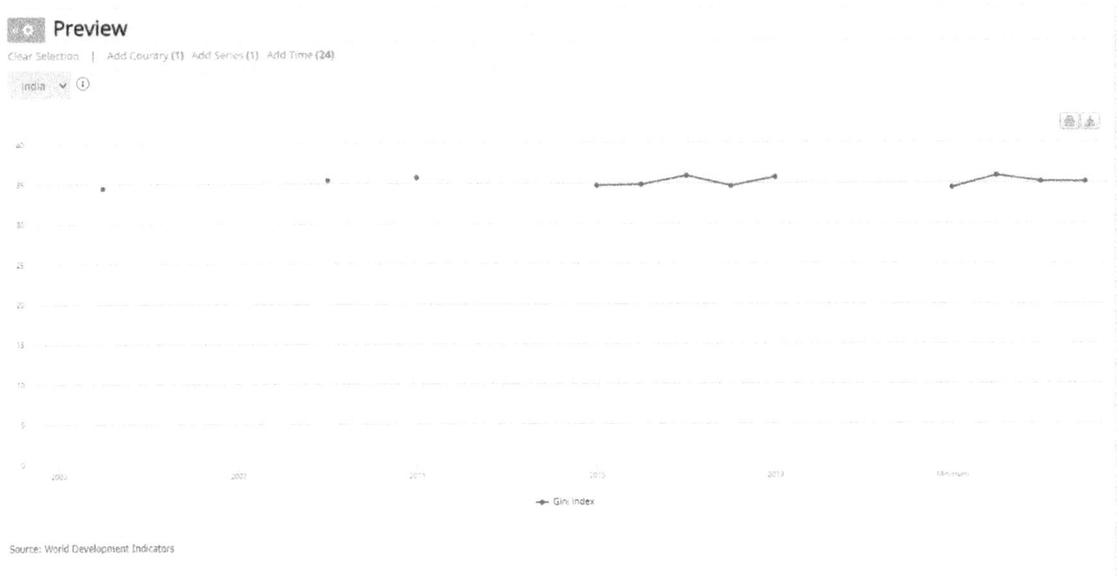

India Gini Index Average **35.1**

(Only 9 data points available for the period 2003-2022)

USA Gini Index average: 40.88
China Gini Index average: 40.33

Sidebar:

Gini coefficient

An indicator designed to measure inequality of income and wealth. It ranges
from zero, which indicates perfect equality, with every household earning or
owning exactly the same, to one, which implies absolute inequality, with a single
household earning a country's entire income or owning all its wealth. African
countries tend to have high Gini coefficients; European countries tend to have low
ones. Among rich countries, America has a relatively high coefficient. Despite
being a notionally communist country, China has a higher coefficient than many
rich countries.

https://www.economist.com/economics-a-to-z#G

Population Exponential Growth Rate 2003-2023

Total Population   **1.25**

Female Population 1.27 % of Total Population 48.41 (2022)
Exponential growth rate of %: 0.02
Male Population   1.24 % of Total Population 51.59 (2022)
Exponential growth rate of %: -0.02

Fertility rate, total (births per woman)

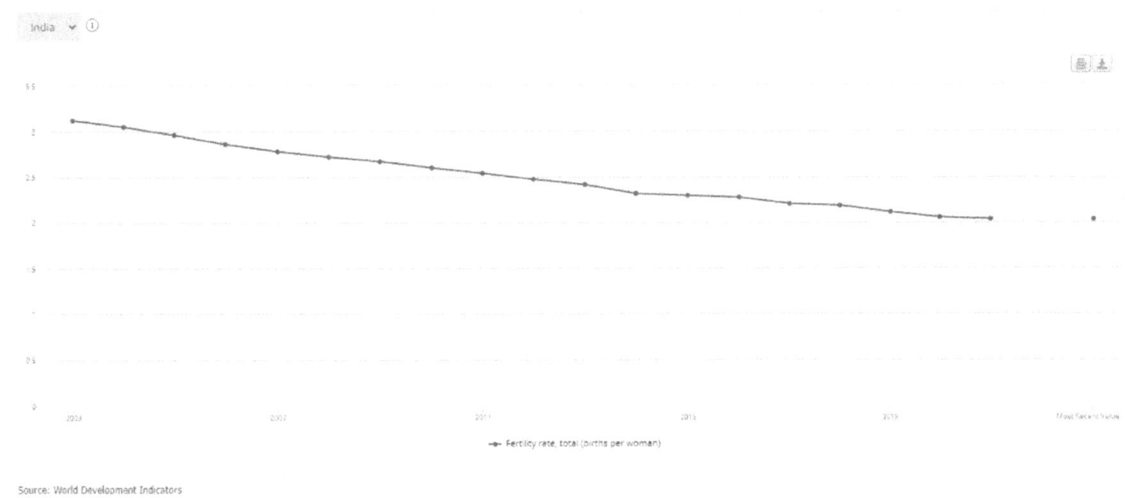

Source: World Development Indicators

Decrease from 2003-2022:   1.02
% Decrease from 2003-2022: 33.40%

Decrease from 2004-2013:   0.64
% Decrease from 2004-2013: 20.98%

Decrease from 2014-2021:   0.28
% Decrease from 2014-2021: 12.12%

Most recent published fertility rate for India is 2.03, nearly the same as the benchmark replacement rate of 2.1 children per woman.

Sidebar

The replacement fertility rate is the average number of children a woman must have to keep the population steady and it is considered to be 2.1 children per woman.

Life expectancy at birth, total (years)

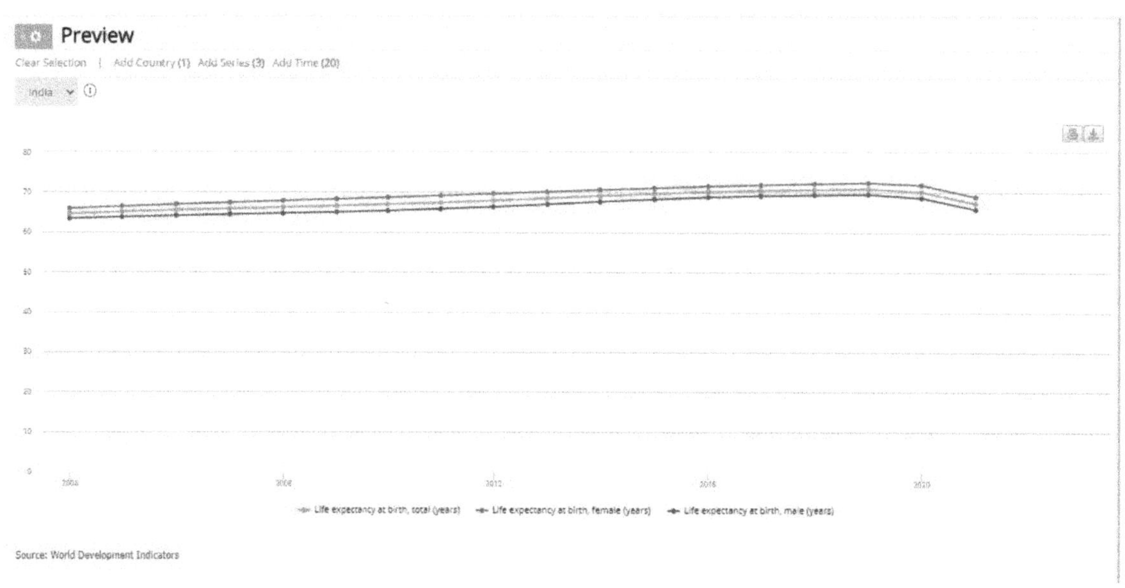

Life expectancy at birth, total (years): 67.24

Life expectancy at birth, female (years): 68.89

Life expectancy at birth, male (years): 65.76

No further analysis was done in view of the impact of COVID-19.

Military expenditure (% of GDP)

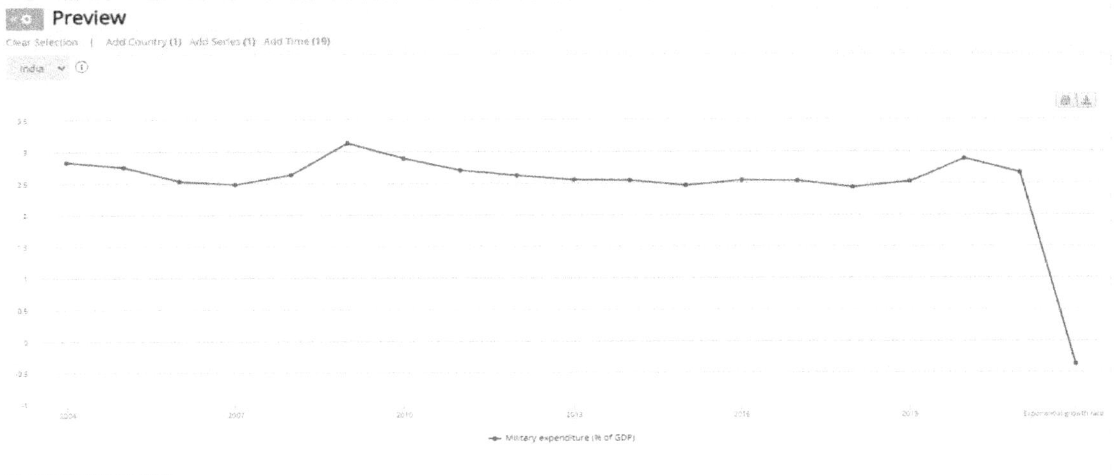

Source: World Development Indicators

2004-2021 Exponential growth rate: -0.37

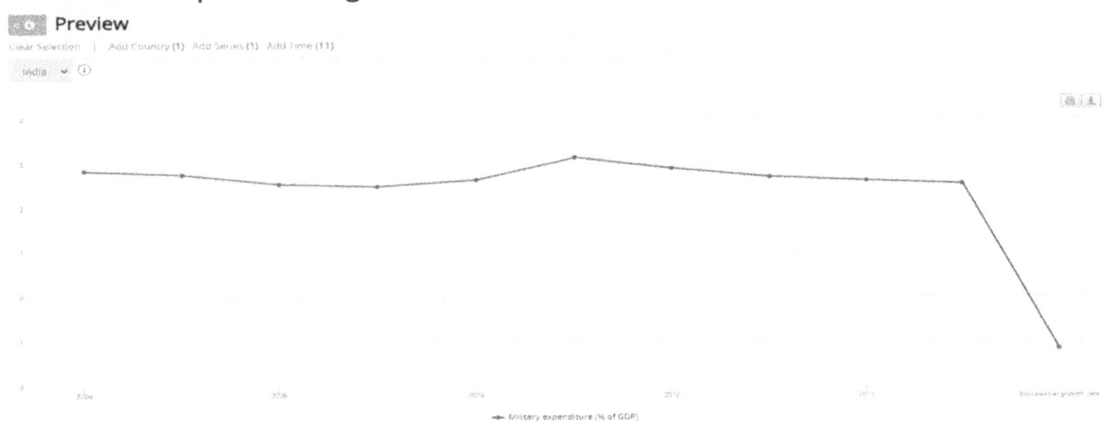

Source: World Development Indicators

2004-

2013 Exponential growth rate:-1.16

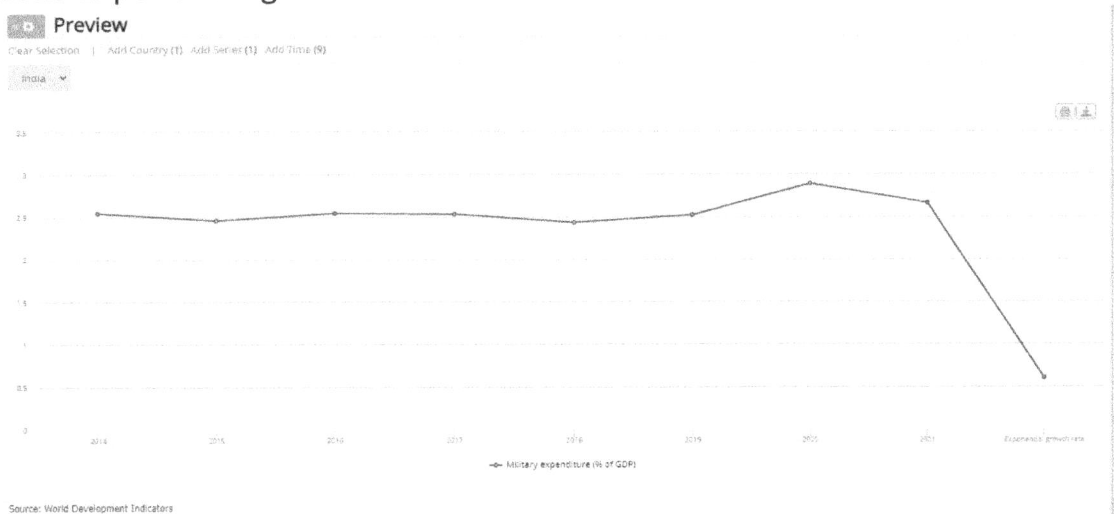

Source: World Development Indicators

2014-2021 Exponential growth rate: 0.6

Inflation, consumer prices (annual %)

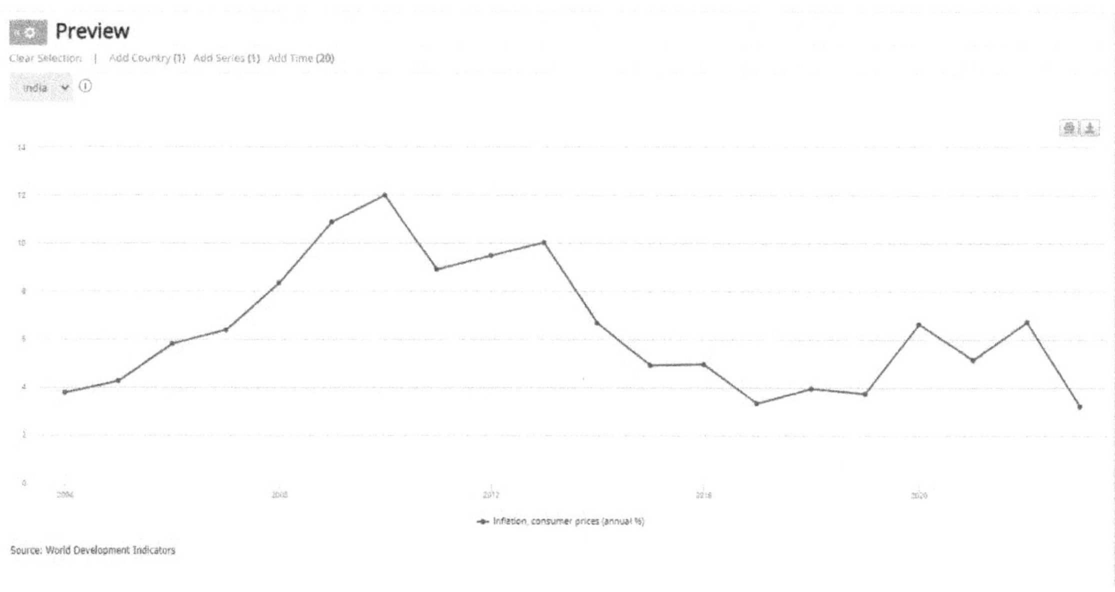

2004-2022 Exponential growth rate: 3.2

India's inflation hits 15-month high

"Inflation rose to 7.44% during the month (July 2023), up sharply from 4.87% in June (2023), putting it at its highest level since April 2022. Food inflation, which accounts for around half of the total consumer basket, jumped to 11.51% in July (2023) – up from just 4.49% in June 2023"

World Economic Forum (https://www.weforum.org)

https://www.weforum.org/agenda/2023/08/india-inflation-interest-rates-economy-news-18-august/#:~:text=Inflation%20rose%20to%207.44%25%20during,from%20just%204.49%25%20in%20June.

Inflation, consumer prices (annual %) (contd.)

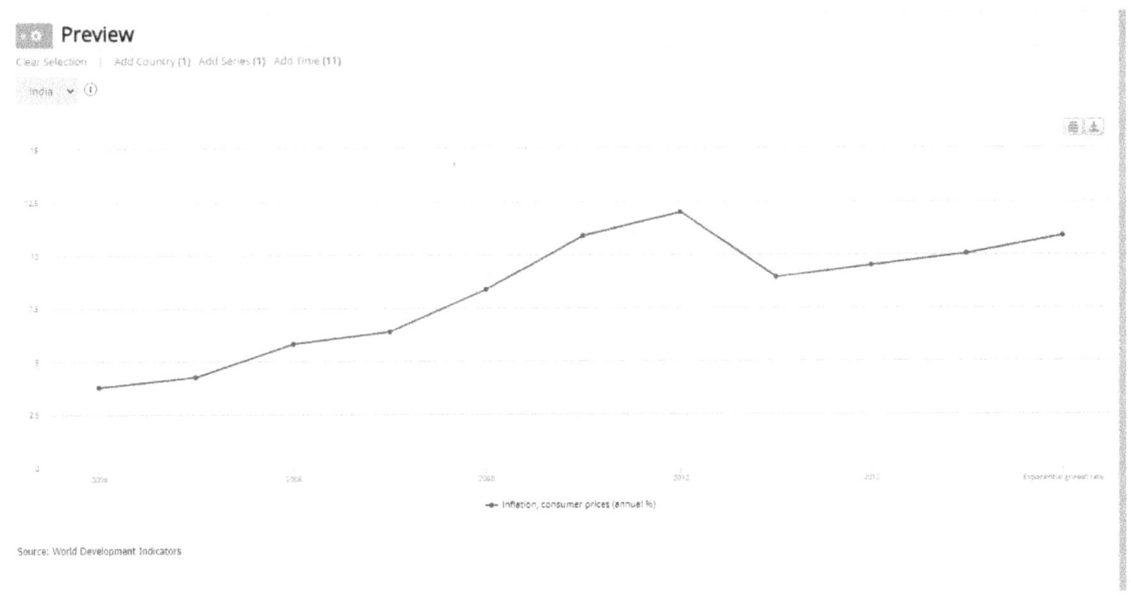

2004-2013 Exponential growth rate: 10.87

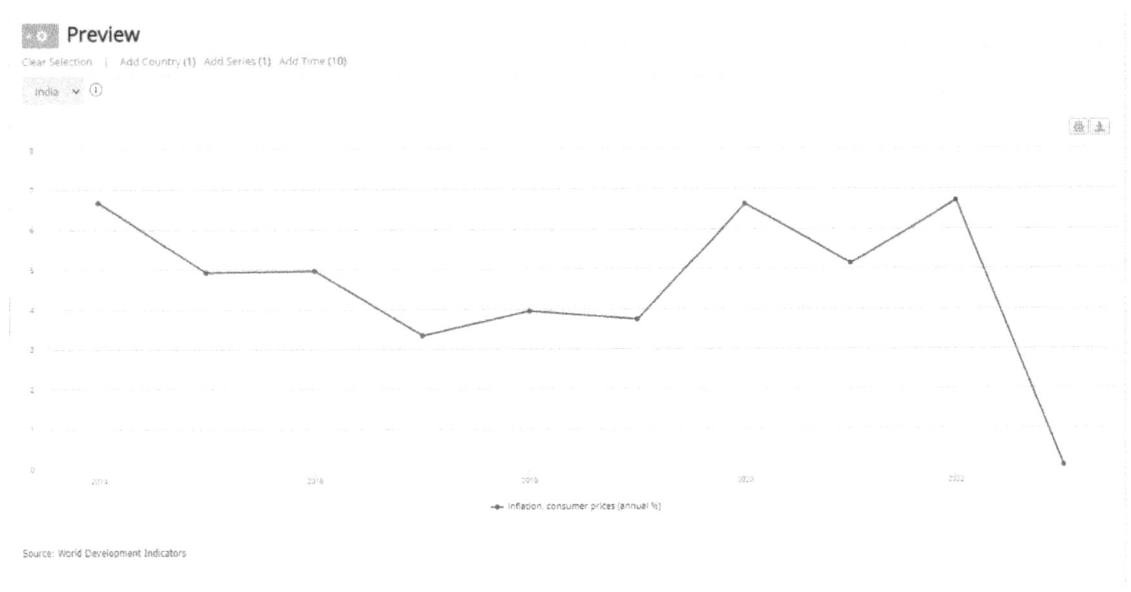

2013-2022 Exponential growth rate: 0.06

As before, the 2008 global melt down and Covid-19 (2019-20) distort the picture.

Urban population (% of total)

Population density (people per sq. km of land area)

CO2 emissions (metric tons per capita)

Health expenditure, total (% of GDP)

Population growth (annual %)

International tourism, number of arrivals

GDP per capita growth (annual %)

Foreign direct investment, net inflows (BoP, current US$)

Government expenditure on education, total (% of GDP)

Literacy rate, adult total (% of people ages 15 and above)

Access to electricity (% of population)

Unemployment, total (% of total labor force) (modeled ILO estimate)

Exports of goods and services (% of GDP)

Mortality rate, infant (per 1,000 live births)

Urban population (% of total)

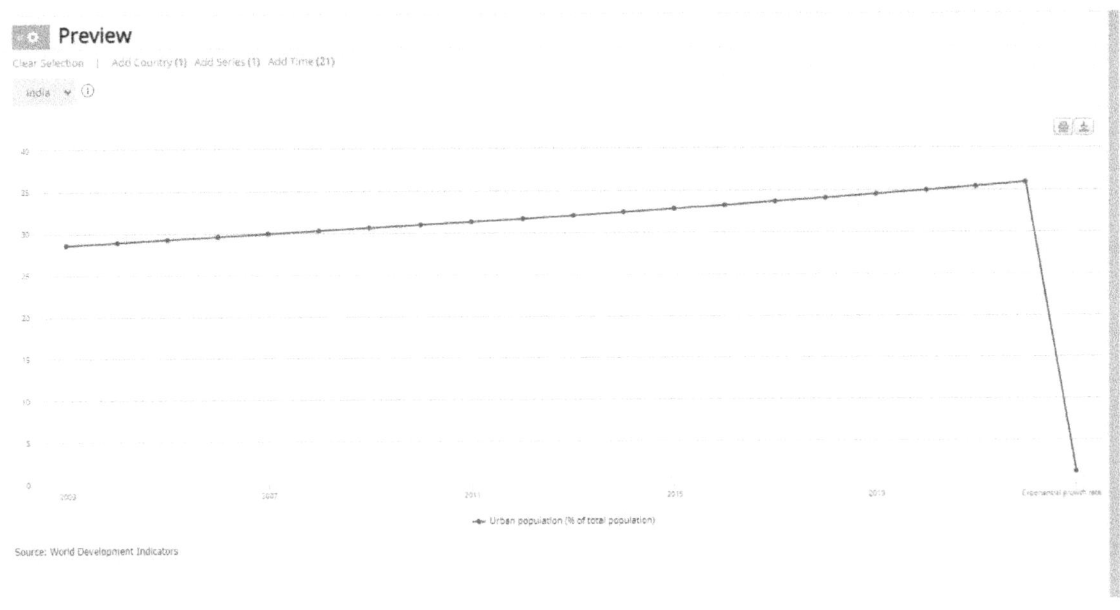

2003-2022 Urban population (% of total) Exponential growth rate: 1.2

Most Recent Value of Urban population (% of total): 35.87%

Population density (people per sq. km of land area)

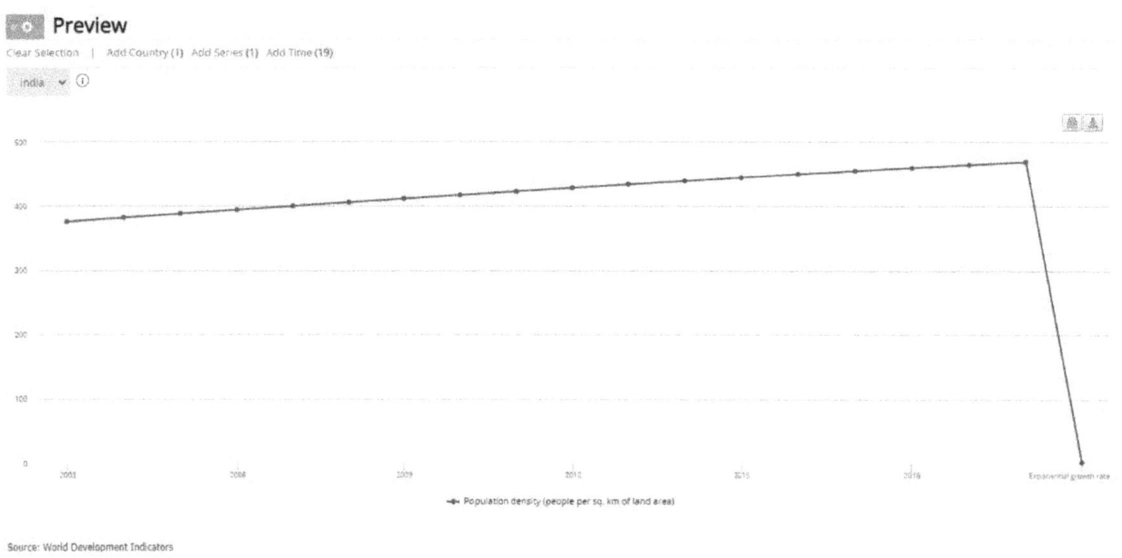

2003 - 2020 Population density (people per sq. km of land area): **1.31**

Most Recent Value: **469.66** (2020)

Sidebar:

Population Rank 1
Growth Rate: 0.86% (118th)
2023 World Percentage: 17.85%
Land Area: 2,973,190
Density: 480.50/km^2 (27th)

The current population of India is **1,430,326,518** (August 2023) based on projections of the latest United Nations data.

Population density (people per sq. km of land area) (contd.,)

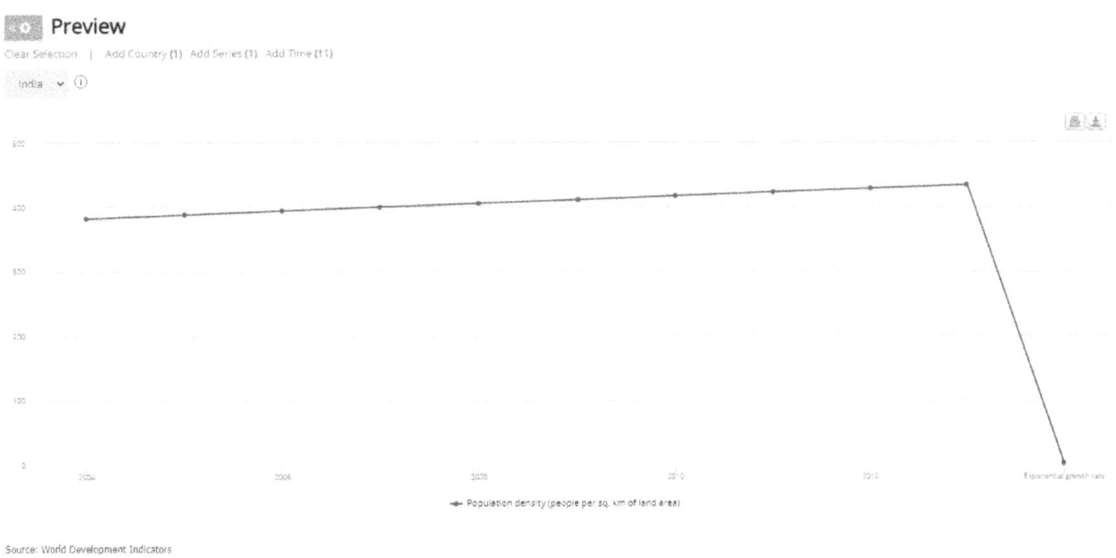

2004-2013 Population density growth rate: **1.42**

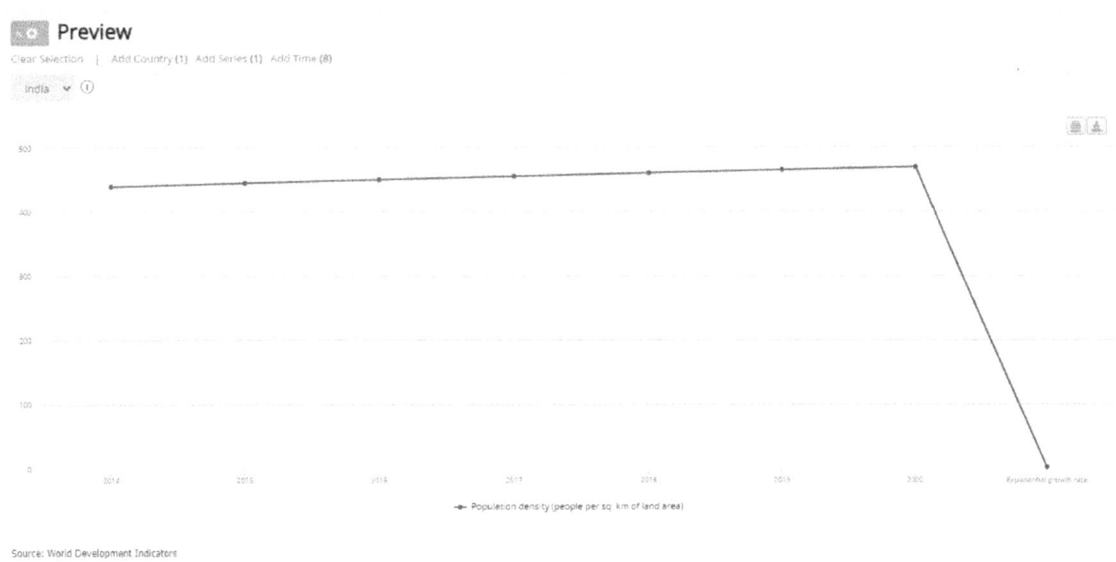

2014-2020 Population density growth rate: **1.1**

<u>CO2 emissions (metric tons per capita)</u>

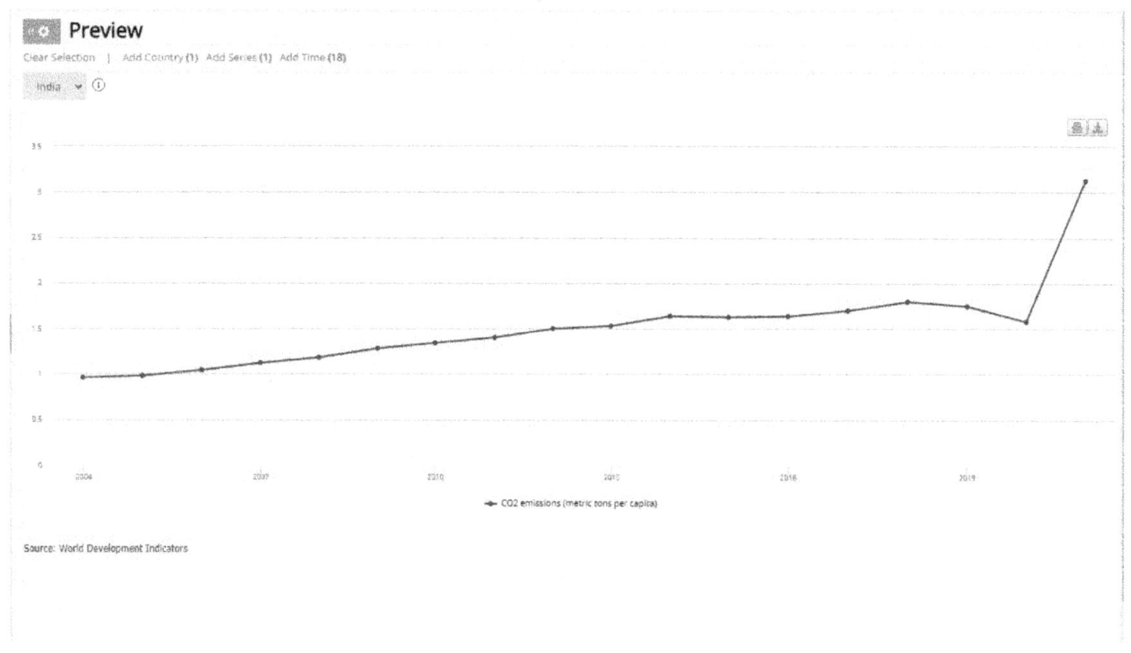

2004-2020 Exponential growth rate: 3.13

CO2 emissions (metric tons per capita) (contd.,)

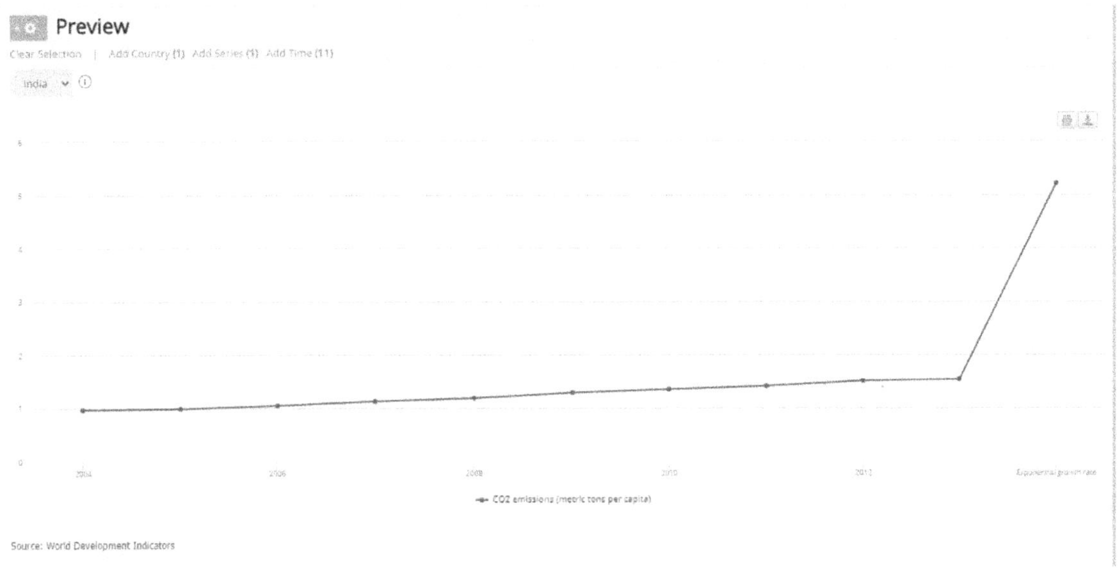

2004-2013 Exponential growth rate: **5.21**

There was no fall after the meltdown.

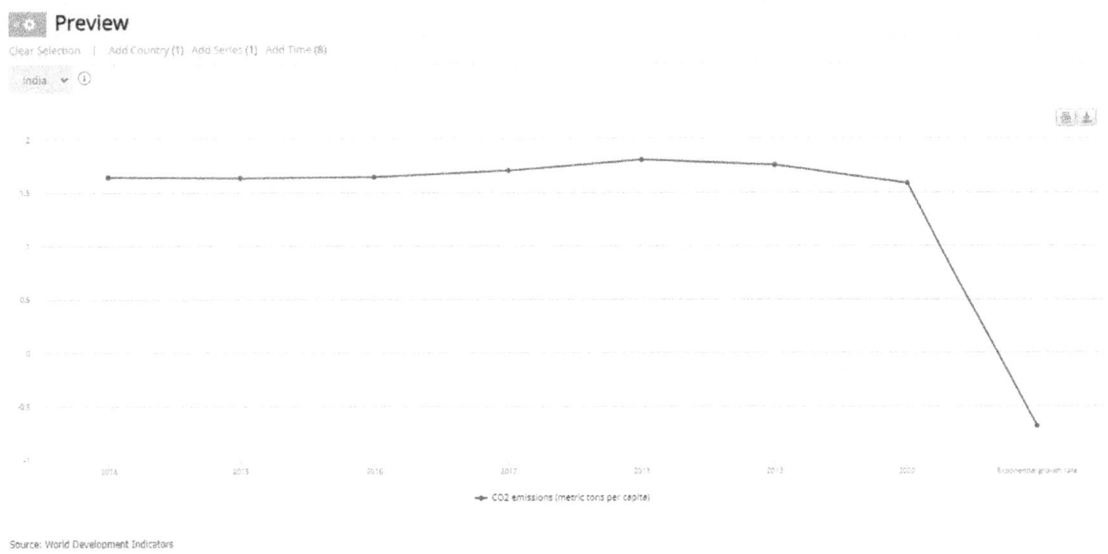

2014-2020 Exponential growth rate: **-0.69**

Sharp fall after Covid-19 (2019-20)

No data available after 2020.

<u>Health expenditure, total (% of GDP)</u>

No data under this head.

International tourism, number of arrivals

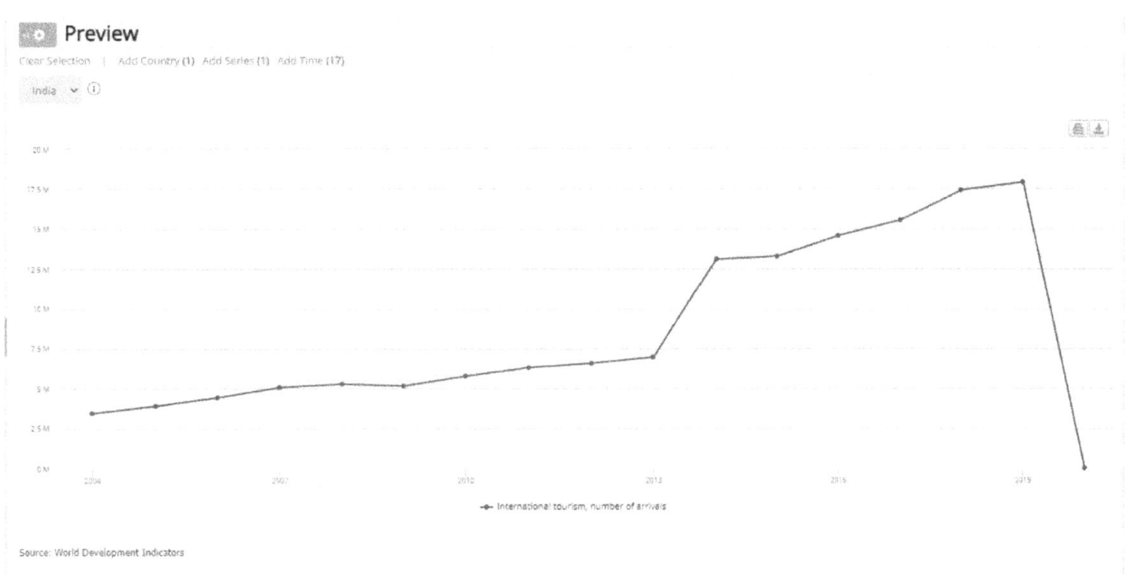

2004-2019 Exponential growth rate: **10.97**

Data not available after 2019 (post Covid-19)

Foreign direct investment, net inflows (BoP, current US$)

Government expenditure on education, total (% of GDP)

Literacy rate, adult total (% of people ages 15 and above)

Access to electricity (% of population)

Unemployment, total (% of total labor force) (modeled ILO estimate)

Exports of goods and services (% of GDP)

Mortality rate, infant (per 1,000 live births)

Foreign direct investment, net inflows (BoP, current US$)

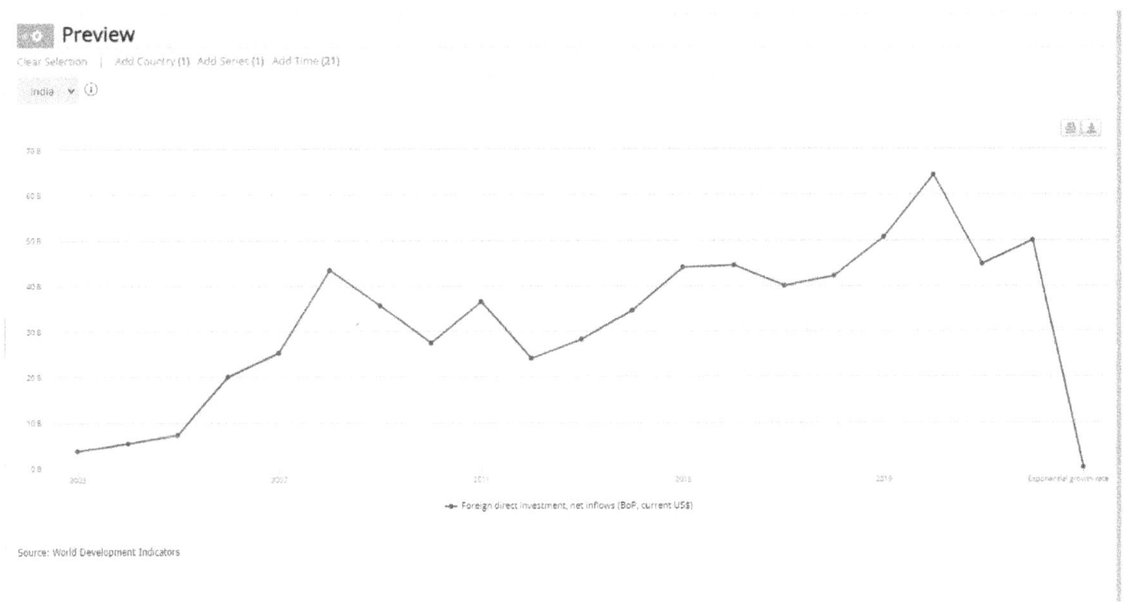

2004-2022 Exponential growth rate:**13.2**

Most recent value: **49,915,506,924.81**

Foreign direct investment, net inflows (BoP, current US$) (contd.,)

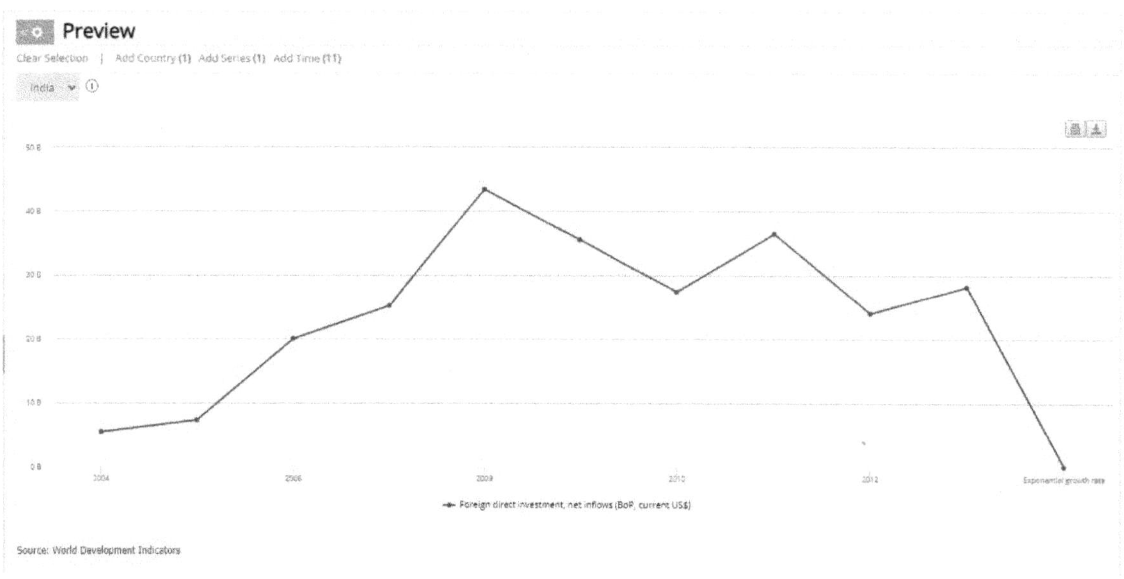

2004-2013 Exponential growth rate: **18.29**

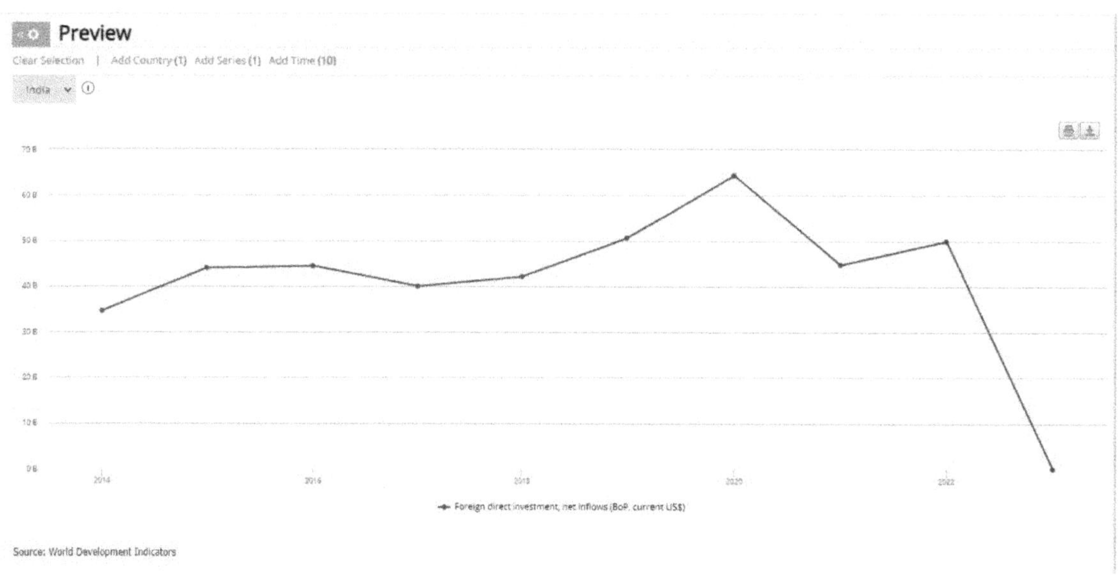

2014-2022 Exponential growth rate: **4.59**

Government expenditure on education, total (% of GDP)

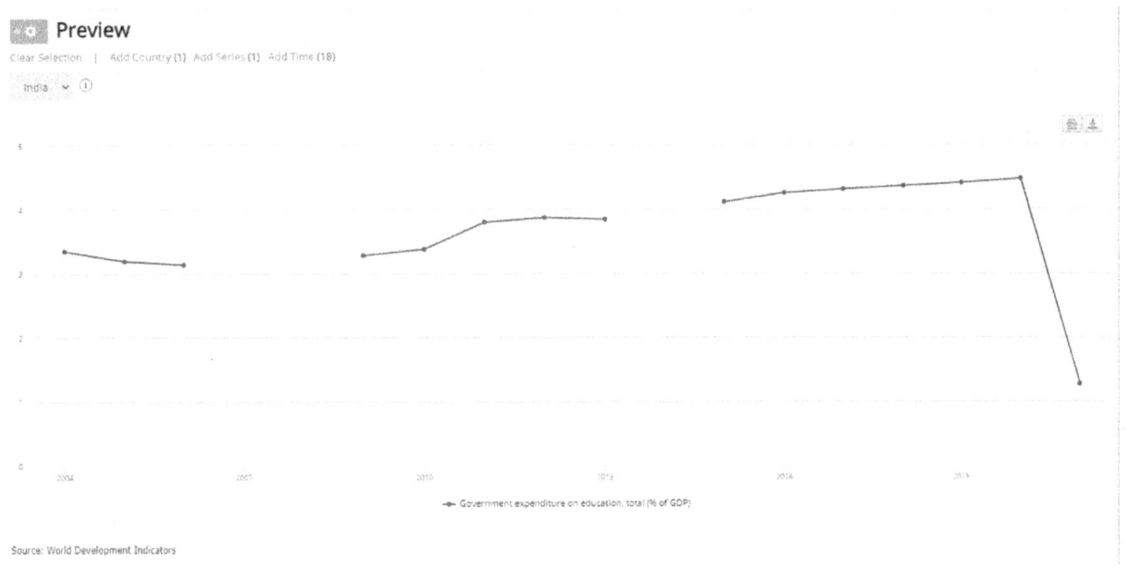

2004 to 2022 Exponential growth rate: **1.26**

Data not available for 2007, 2008 and 2014

Government expenditure on education, total (% of GDP) (contd.,)

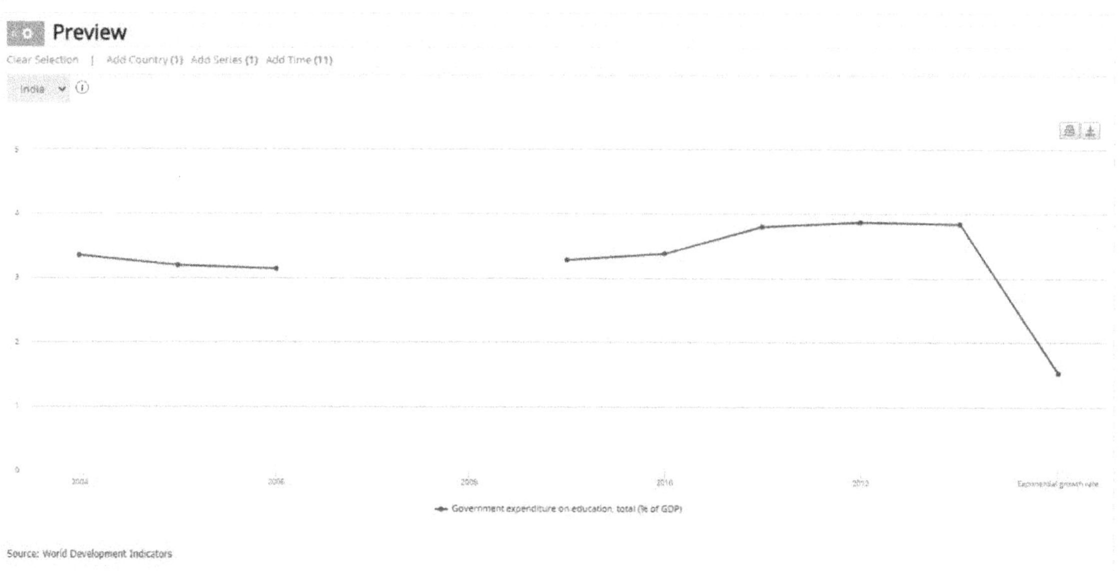

2004-2013 Exponential growth rate: **1.52**

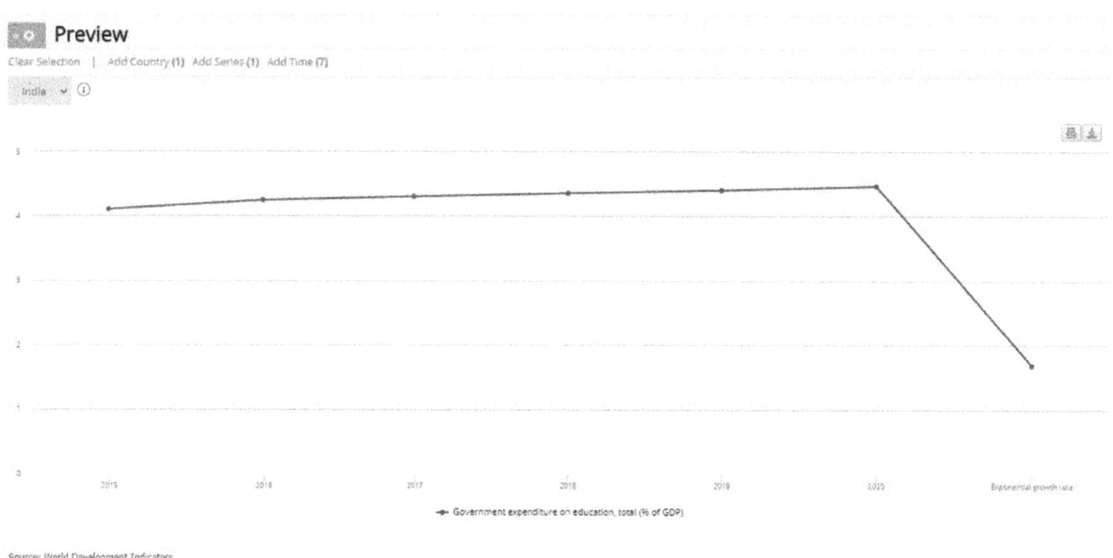

2015-2020 Exponential growth rate: **1.68**

No data available for 2014 and after 2020

Literacy rate, adult total (% of people ages 15 and above)

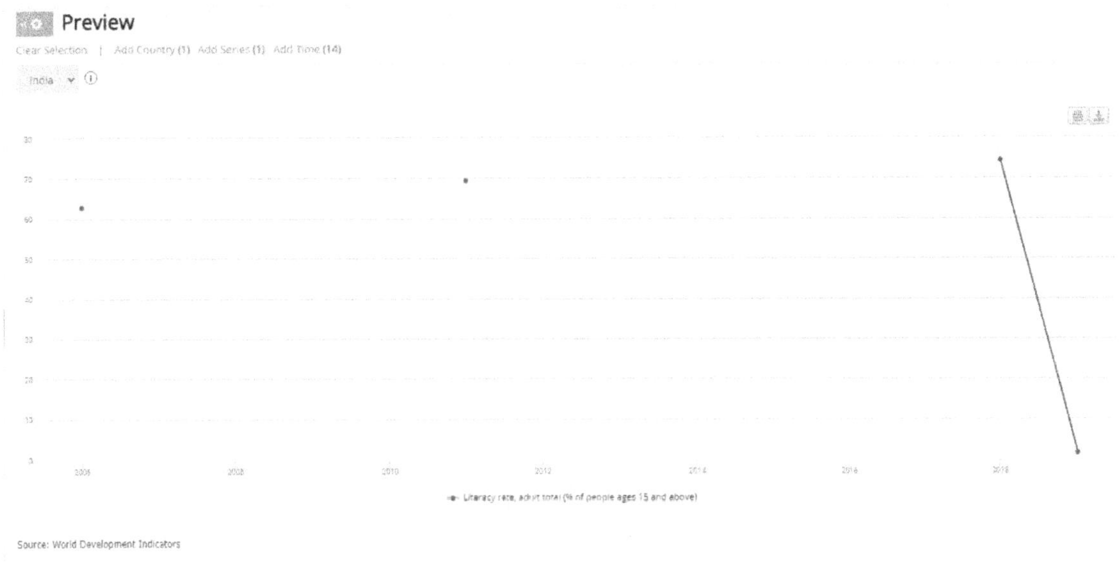

2006-2018 Exponential growth rate: **1.42**

Only 3 data points are available.

Access to electricity (% of population)

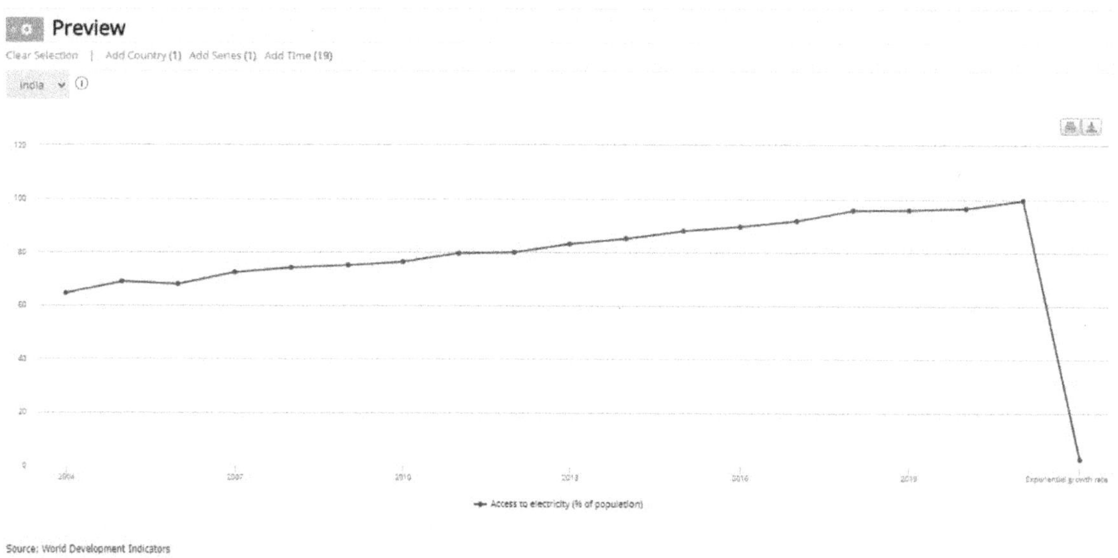

2004-2021 Exponential growth rate: **2.56**

Most Recent Value: 99.57 (2021)

Access to electricity (% of population) (contd.,)

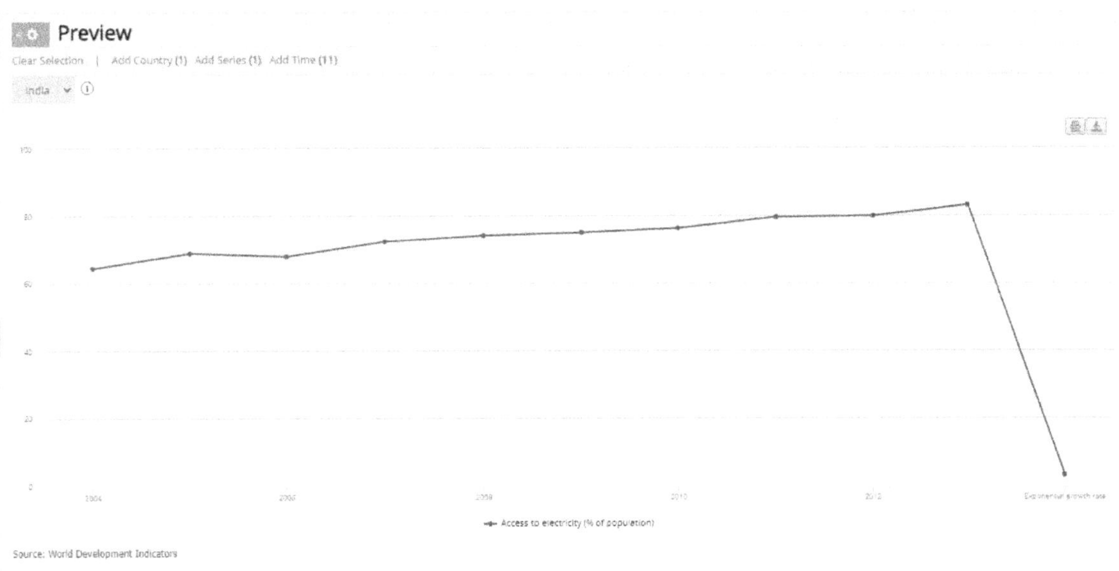

2004-2013 Exponential growth rate: **2.84**

2014 Access to electricity (% of population):   85.13

2004 Access to electricity (% of population):   64.40

Addition to access to electricity (% of population): **20.73**

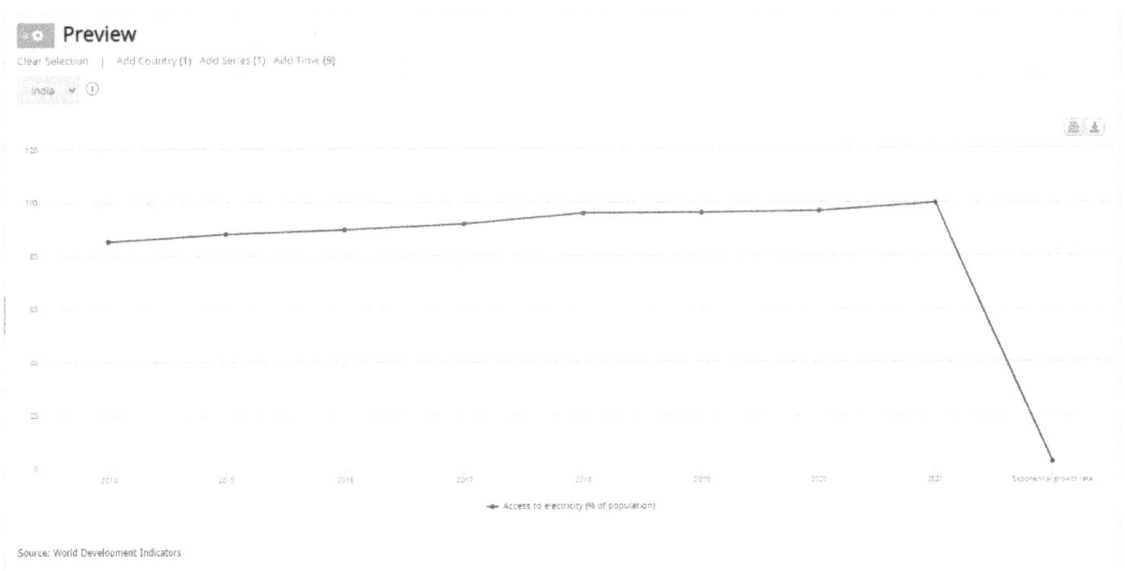

2014-2021 Exponential growth rate: **2.24**

2021 Access to electricity (% of population):   99.57

2014 Access to electricity (% of population):   85.13

Addition to access to electricity (% of population):**14.44**

<u>Mortality rate, infant (per 1,000 live births)</u>

Unemployment, total (% of total labor force)
(modeled ILO estimate)

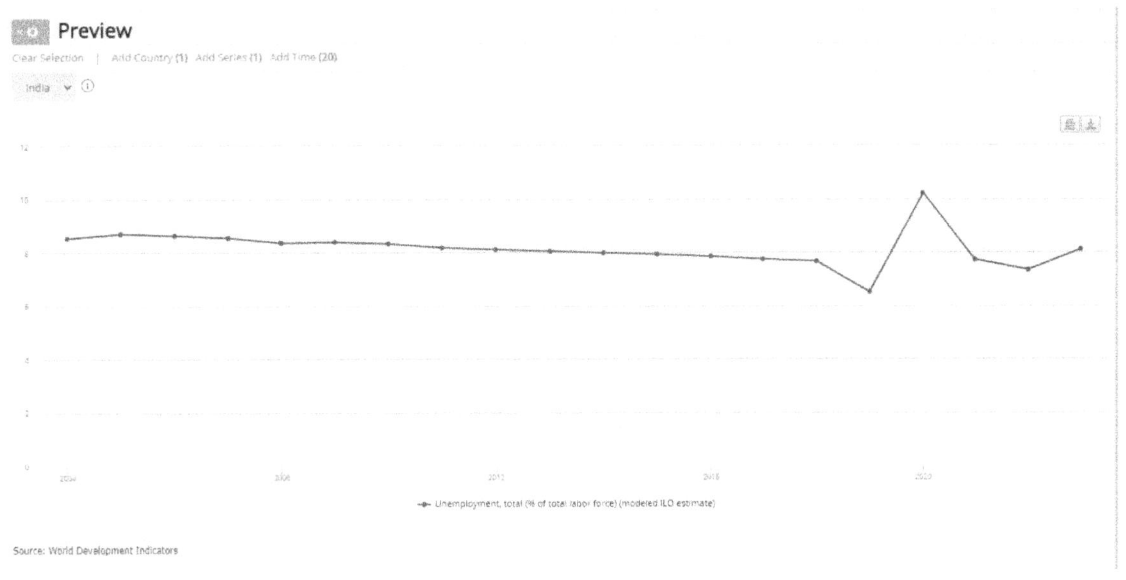

2004-2022 Unemployment, total (% of total labor force): **8.1**

Unemployment, total (% of total labor force) (modeled ILO estimate)

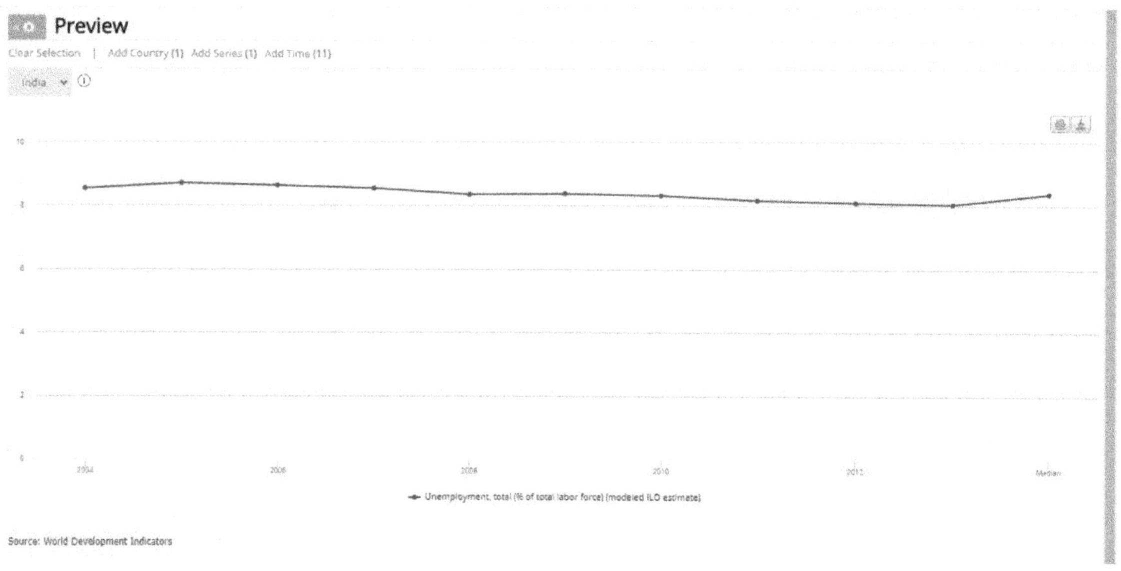

2004-2013 Median **8.37**

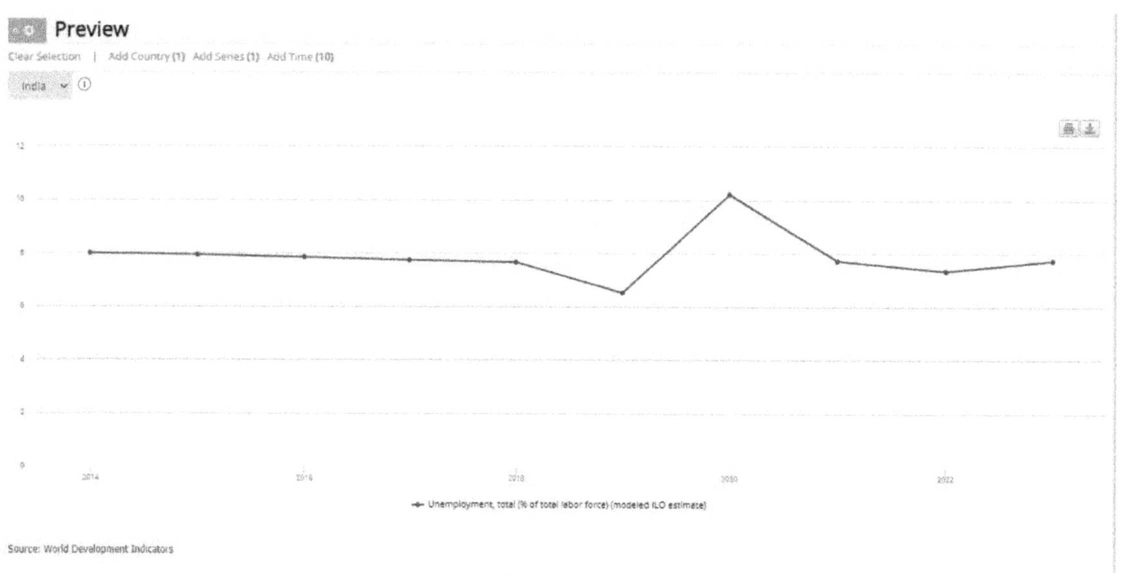

2014-2022 Median **7.73**

Exports of goods and services (% of GDP)

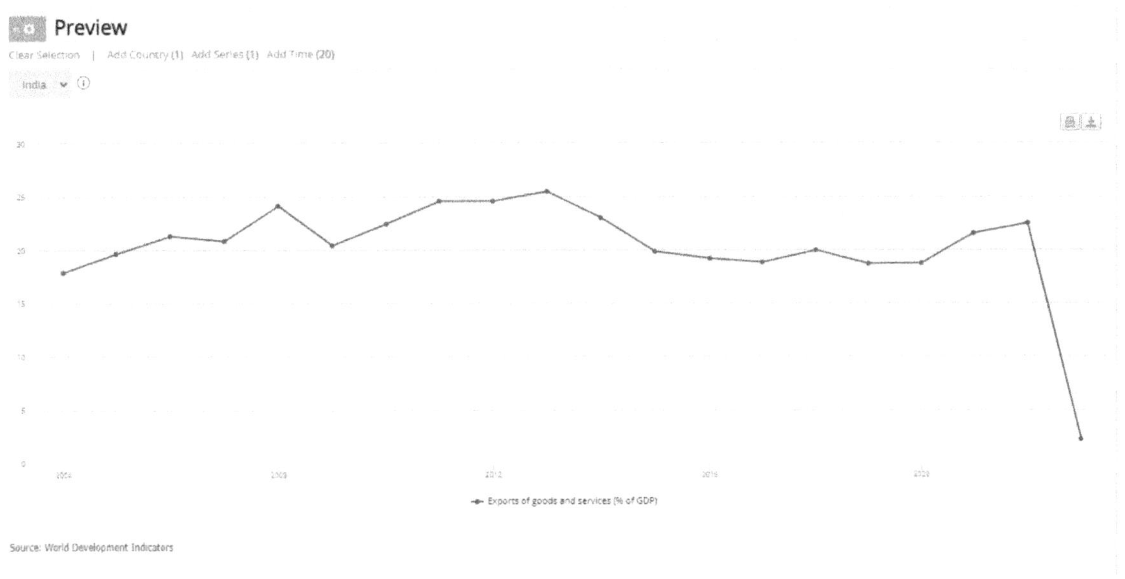

2004-2022 Exponential growth rate: **2.14**

Exports of goods and services (% of GDP) (contd.,)

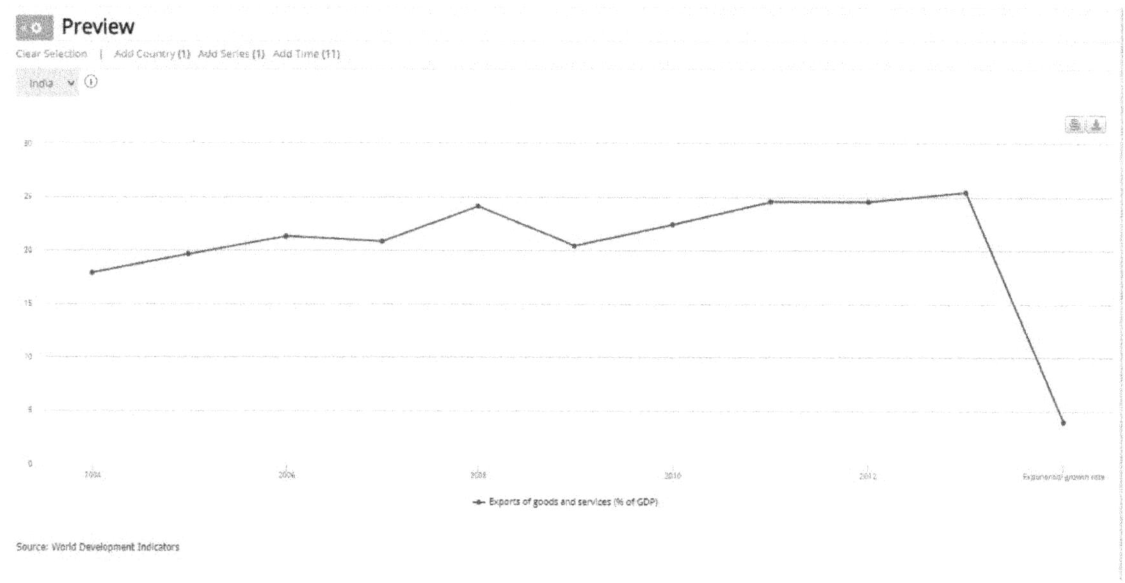

2004-2013 Exponential growth rate: **3.93**

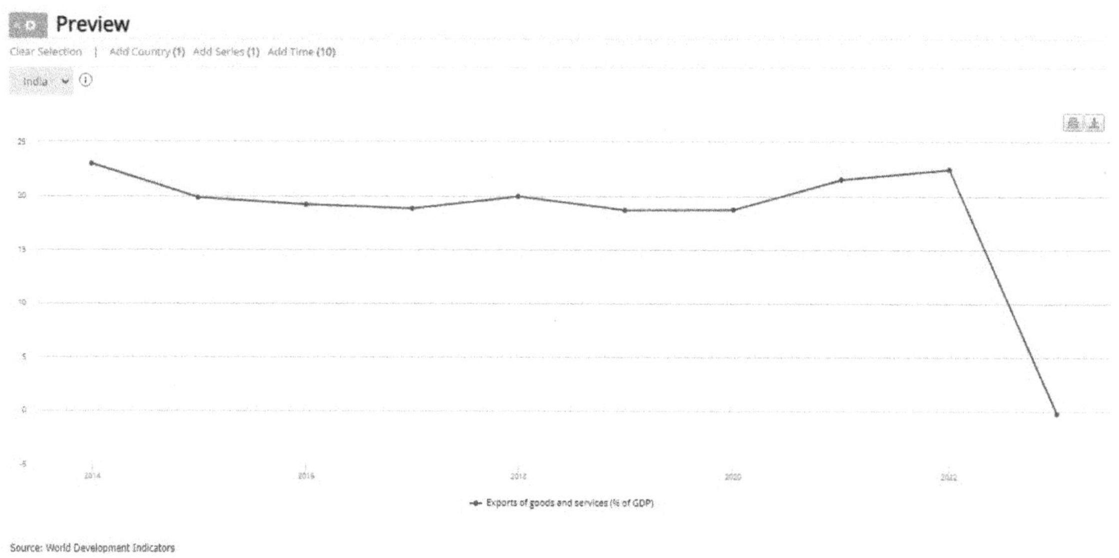

2014-2023 Exponential growth rate: -0.29

Mortality rate, infant (per 1,000 live births)

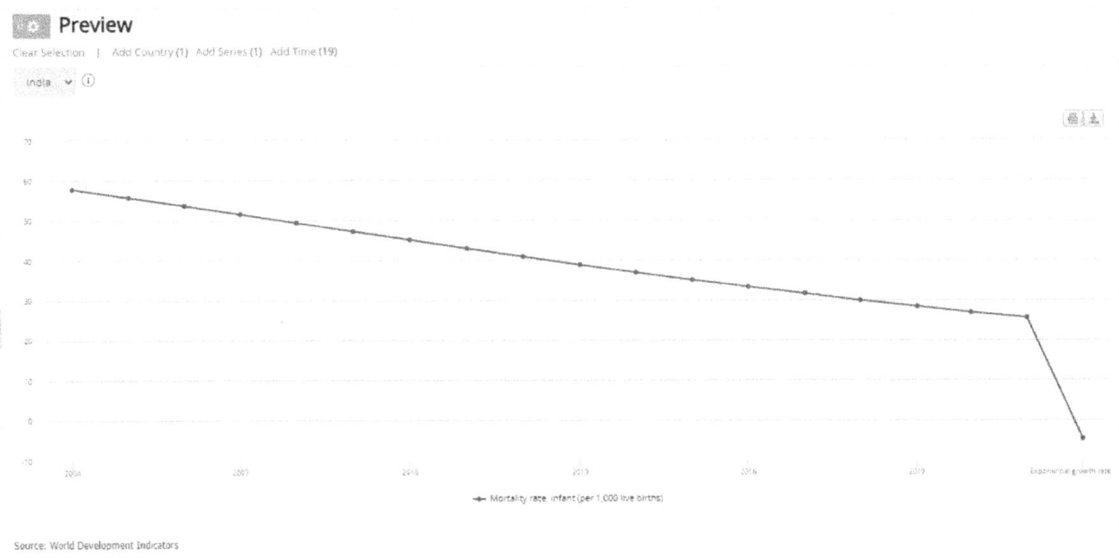

2004-2022 Exponential growth rate: -4.81

Mortality rate, infant (per 1,000 live births)

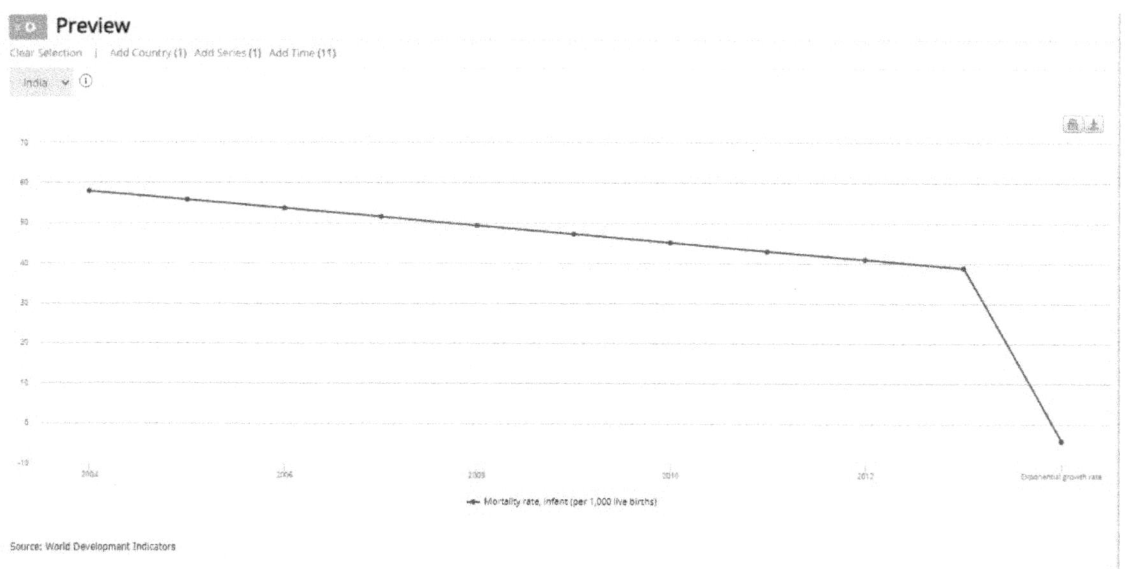

2004-2013: Exponential growth rate: **-4.43**

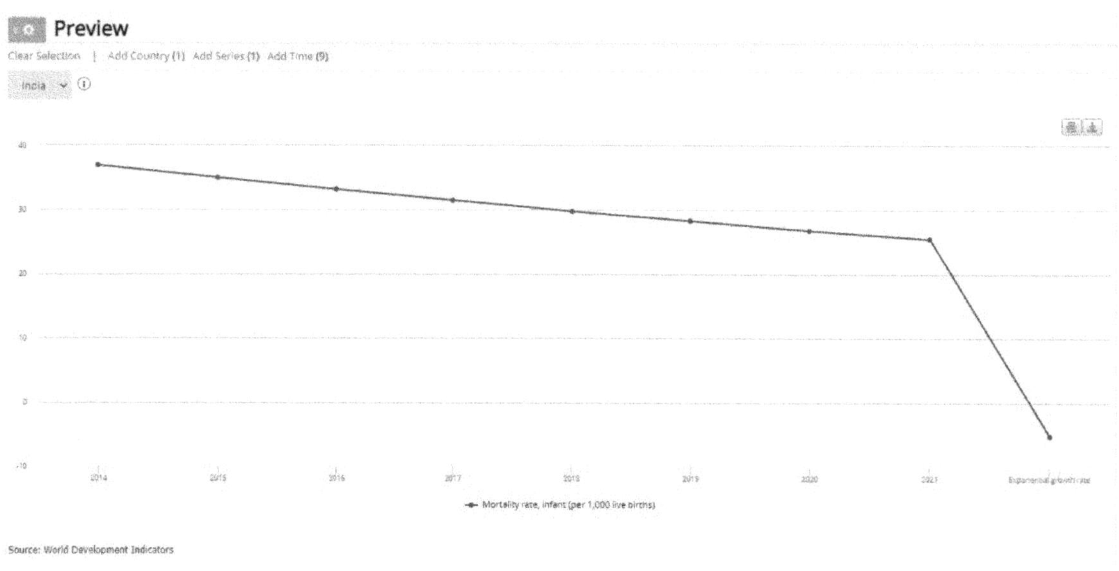

2004-2013: Exponential growth rate: **-5.28**

OTHER GLOBAL INDICES

A short list of Key Indices

1. Human Development Index (HDI): Measures a country's overall development based on life expectancy, education, and per capita income.

2. Global Hunger Index (GHI): Assesses the level of hunger and under-nutrition in a country based on factors like undernourishment, child wasting, child stunting, and child mortality.

3. World Happiness Report: Ranks countries based on factors like income, social support, life expectancy, freedom to make life choices, trust, and generosity.

4. Gender Gap Index: Measures gender-based disparities in areas such as economic participation, educational attainment, health, and political empowerment.

5. Global Peace Index (GPI): Ranks countries based on their level of peace and stability, considering factors such as ongoing conflicts, societal safety, and political stability.

6. Perceptions Index (CPI): Assesses the perceived level of public sector corruption in a country, based on expert opinions and surveys.

7. Ease of Doing Business Index: Evaluates the business regulatory environment in terms of starting and operating a business in a country.

8. Environmental Performance Index (EPI): Ranks countries on their environmental performance based on indicators like air quality, water and sanitation, biodiversity, and climate change.

9. Inequality-adjusted Human Development Index (IHDI): A modification of the HDI that takes into account inequality in addition to the standard HDI factors.

10. Global Innovation Index (GII): Assesses a country's innovation capabilities and outcomes based on factors like research and development investments, intellectual property protection, and technological achievements.

11. World Economic Forum's Global Competitiveness Index: Ranks countries based on factors that contribute to their economic competitiveness and growth.

12. World Bank's Doing Business Report: Offers insights into business regulations and their enforcement across economies.

13. OECD Better Life Index: Allows users to compare well-being across countries based on various indicators like housing, income, jobs, community, education, environment, governance, health, life satisfaction, safety, and work-life balance.

14. Global Slavery Index: Estimates the prevalence of modern slavery in terms of human trafficking, forced labor, and other forms of exploitation.

15. Global Terrorism Index (GTI): Measures the impact and trends of terrorism on a global scale.

Human Development Index (HDI)

https://www.undp.org/india/press-releases/india-ranks-132-human-development-index-global-development-stalls

India ranks 132 on the Human Development Index as global development stalls
SEPTEMBER 8, 2022

INDIA RANKS 132 OUT OF 191 COUNTRIES AND TERRITORIES ON THE 2021/22 HUMAN DEVELOPMENT INDEX

The Global Hunger Index

https://www.globalhungerindex.org/2023.html

The Global Hunger Index (GHI) measures and tracks the hunger situation at global, regional and national levels over the long term, and is jointly published by Welthungerhilfe and Concern Worldwide since 2006.

The 2023 edition will be published in October 2023.

Welthungerhilfe is one of the largest non-governmental development and humanitarian aid organizations in Germany, fighting for ''Zero Hunger by 2030''.

Concern Worldwide is a non-governmental, international, humanitarian organization working towards the ultimate elimination of extreme poverty in the world's poorest countries.

https://www.globalhungerindex.org/pdf/en/2022.pdf

India's Hunger Index Score is 29.1 and is ranked at 107 out of 121 countries.

Computation methodology image on the following page.

Components of HDI

 ABOUT THE GLOBAL HUNGER INDEX SCORES

The Global Hunger Index (GHI) is a tool for comprehensively measuring and tracking hunger at global, regional, and national levels. GHI scores are based on the values of four component indicators:[3]

 **Undernourishment:** the share of the population with insufficient caloric intake.

 **Child wasting:** the share of children under age five who have low weight for their height, reflecting *acute* undernutrition.

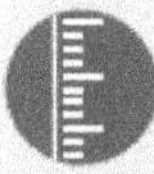 **Child stunting:** the share of children under age five who have low height for their age, reflecting *chronic* undernutrition.

 **Child mortality:** the share of children who die before their fifth birthday, partly reflecting the fatal mix of inadequate nutrition and unhealthy environments.

These four indicators are aggregated as follows:

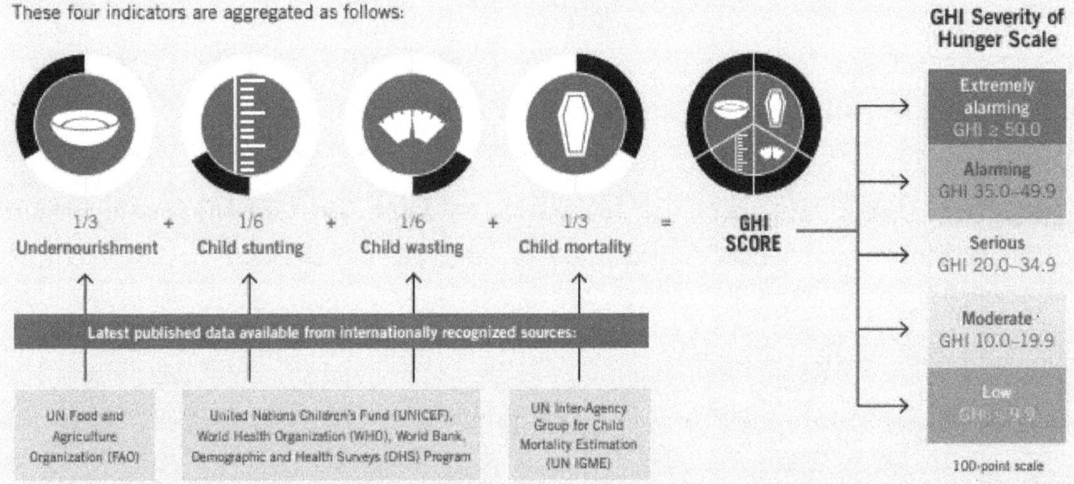

Based on the values of the four indicators, a GHI score is calculated on a 100-point scale reflecting the severity of hunger, where 0 is the best possible score (no hunger) and 100 is the worst.[4] Each country's GHI score is classified by severity, from *low* to *extremely alarming*.

[3] Each of the indicators is standardized; see Appendix A for details.

[4] GHI scores are comparable only within each year's report, not between different years' reports. To allow for tracking of a country's or region's GHI performance over time, this report provides GHI scores for 2000, 2007, and 2014, which can be compared with 2022 GHI scores. For a detailed explanation of the concept of the GHI, the date ranges and calculation of the scores, and the interpretation of results, see Appendix A.

World Happiness Report 2023

https://worldhappiness.report/about/

India ranks at 126th position out of 136 countries.

Life evaluations from the Gallup World Poll provide the basis for the annual happiness rankings. They are based on answers to the main life evaluation question. The Cantril ladder asks respondents to think of a ladder, with the best possible life for them being a 10 and the worst possible life being a 0. They are then asked to rate their own current lives on that 0 to 10 scale. The rankings are from nationally representative samples over three years.

The Six variables that determine the rankings are GDP per capita, social support, healthy life expectancy, freedom, generosity, and corruption.

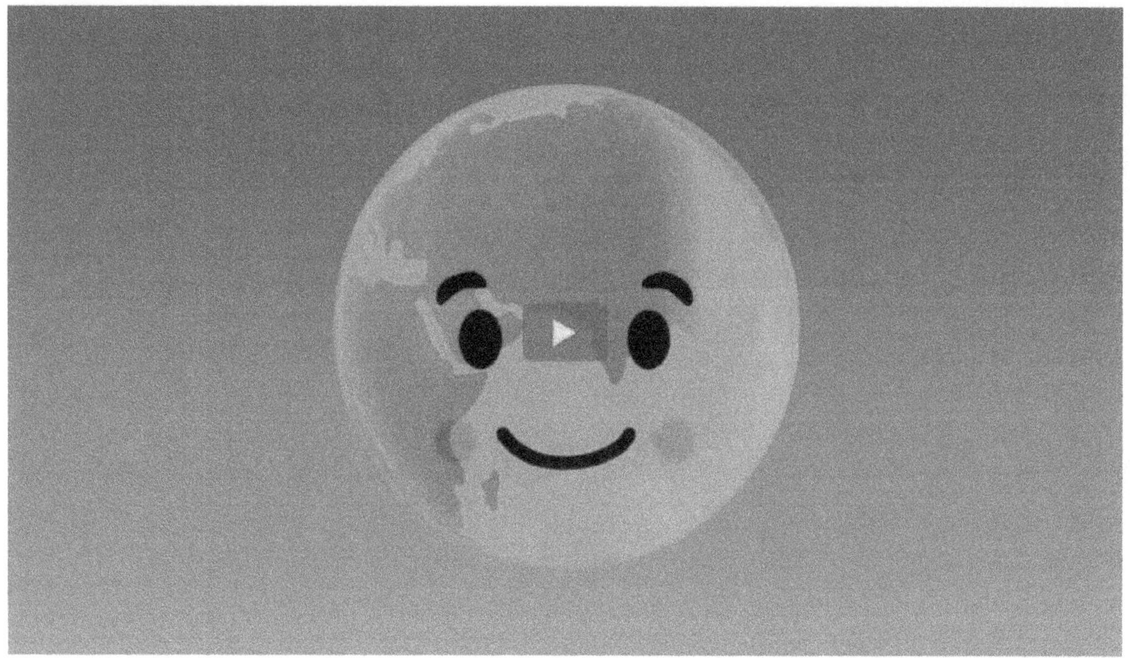

World Happiness Day March 2023 Theme:

Be Mindful, Be Grateful, Be Kind

Gender Gap

https://www.weforum.org/reports/global-gender-gap-report-2023/

Global Gender Gap Report 2023

The Global Gender Gap Index annually benchmarks the current state and evolution of gender parity across four key dimensions (Economic Participation and Opportunity, Educational Attainment, Health and Survival, and Political Empowerment). It is the longest-standing index tracking the progress of numerous countries' efforts towards closing these gaps over time since its inception in 2006.

India has been ranked at 127 out of 146 countries.

Global Peace Index (GPI)

Produced by the <u>Institute for Economics and Peace</u> (IEP), the Global Peace Index (GPI) is the world's leading measure of global peacefulness. This report presents the most comprehensive data-driven analysis to-date on trends in peace, its economic value, and how to develop peaceful societies.

The Global Peace Index covers 99.7% of the world's population, and is calculated using <u>23 qualitative and quantitative indicators</u> from highly respected sources, and measures the state of peace across three domains – the level of Societal Safety and Security, the extent of Ongoing Domestic and International Conflict, and the degree of Militarisation.

<u>https://www.visionofhumanity.org/</u>

Overall Score

2.31

Country Ranking

126 / 163

Global Average

2.314 / 5

A composite index measuring the peacefulness of countries made up of 23 quantitative and qualitative indicators each weighted on a scale of 1-5. The lower the score the more peaceful the country.

(Map on the next page)

GPI World Map

Overall score 2023

https://www.visionofhumanity.org/maps/#/

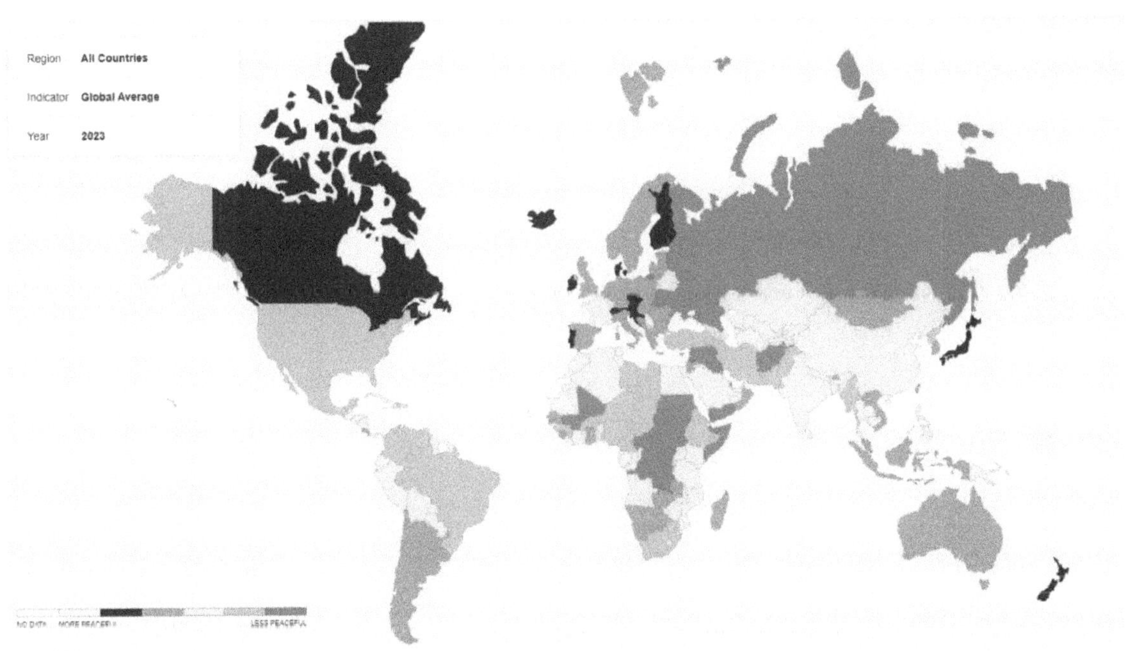

Corruption Perceptions Index (CPI)

The Corruption Perceptions Index (CPI) is an index which ranks countries "by their perceived levels of public sector corruption, as determined by expert assessments and opinion surveys." The CPI generally defines corruption as an "abuse of entrusted power for private gain".

The index is published annually by the non-governmental organisation Transparency International since 1995.

The 2022 CPI, published in January 2023, currently ranks 180 countries "on a scale from 100 (very clean) to 0 (highly corrupt)" based on the situation between 1 May 2021 and 30 April 2022.

https://www.transparency.org/en/cpi/2022

A country's score is the perceived level of public sector corruption on a scale of 0-100, where 0 means highly corrupt and 100 means very clean.

A country's rank is its position relative to the other countries in the index. Ranks can change merely if the number of countries included in the index changes.

The rank is therefore not as important as the score in terms of indicating the level of corruption in that country.

INDIA: **Score 40/100 Rank 85/180**

(Map on next page)

Corruption Perceptions Index (CPI) (contd.,)

Score changes 2012-2022

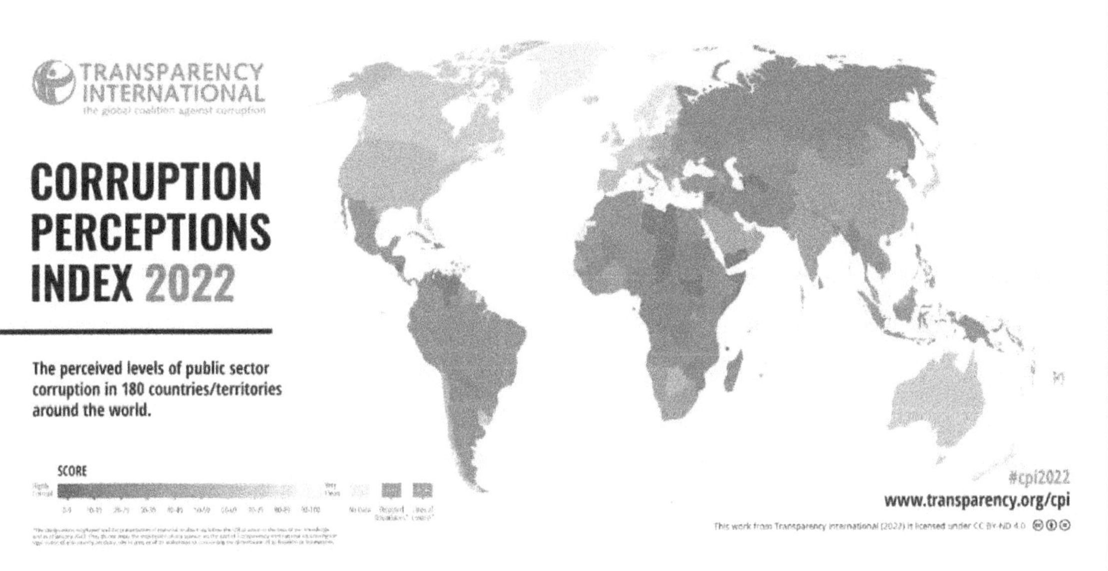

Ease of Doing Business Index

Economies are ranked on their ease of doing business, from 1 −190. A high ease of doing business ranking means the regulatory environment is more conducive to the starting and operation of a local firm. The rankings are determined by sorting the aggregate scores on 10 topics, each consisting of several indicators, giving equal weight to each topic. The rankings for all economies are bench marked to May 2019.

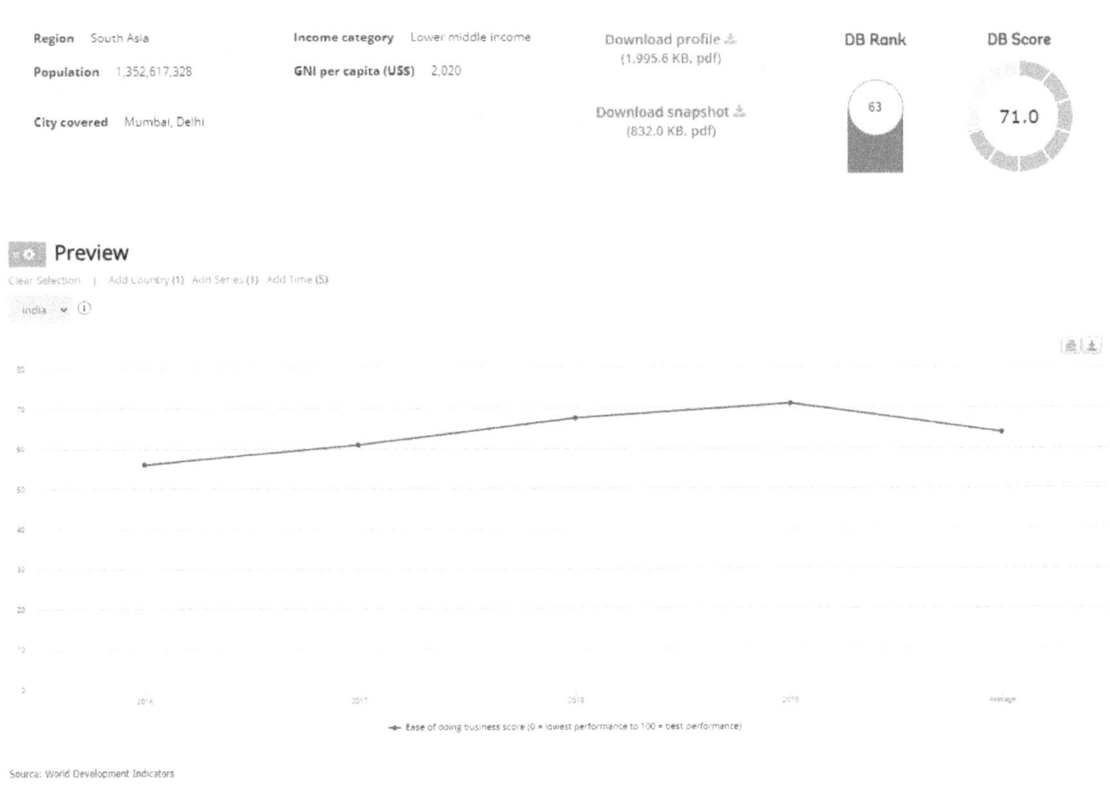

Scanty data - Very few data points.

Average for the period 2016-2019: 63.85%

https://databank.worldbank.org/source/world-development-indicators

https://epi.yale.edu/epi-results/2022/component/epi

The 2022 EPI provides a quantitative basis for comparing, analyzing, and understanding environmental performance for 180 countries. We score and rank these countries on their environmental performance using the most recent year of data available and calculate how these scores have changed over the previous decade.

India Country Report

EPI Rank: 180
EPI Score: 18.90
10-year change: -0.6o

There are several components of EPI, too many to discuss here.

The report is comprehensive and is a wake up call for policymakers and leaders.

https://epi.yale.edu/epi-results/2022/component/epi

INEQUALITY-ADJUSTED HUMAN DEVELOPMENT INDEX (IHDI)

IHDI adjusts the Human Development Index (HDI) for inequality in the distribution of each dimension across the population.

https://hdr.undp.org/inequality-adjusted-human-development-index#/indicies/IHDI

IHDI is based on a distribution-sensitive class of composite indices proposed by Foster, Lopez-Calva and Szekely (2005), which draws on the Atkinson (1970) family of inequality measures. It is computed as a geometric mean of inequality-adjusted dimensional indices. The IHDI accounts for inequalities in HDI dimensions by "discounting" each dimension's average value according to its level of inequality. The IHDI value equals the HDI value when there is no inequality across people but falls below the HDI value as inequality rises. In this sense, the IHDI measures the level of human development when inequality is accounted for.

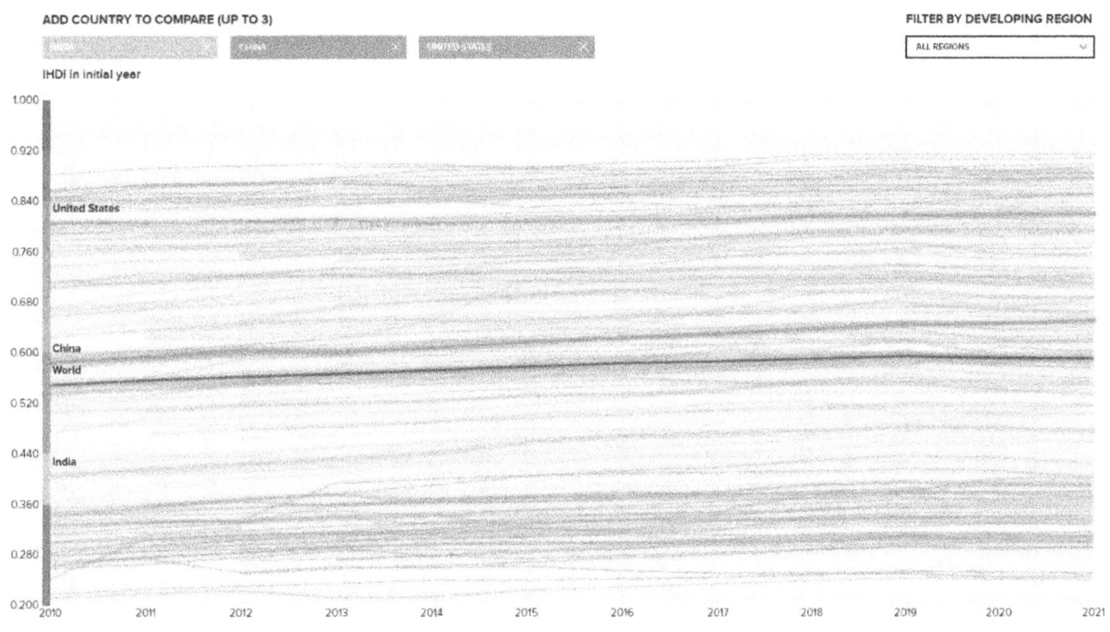

Global Innovation Index (GII)

Assesses a country's innovation capabilities and outcomes based on factors like research and development investments, intellectual property protection, and technological achievements.

https://www.wipo.int/global_innovation_index/en/news/2023/index.html

The World Intellectual Property Organization (WIPO) is the global forum for intellectual property (IP) services, policy, information and cooperation. We are a self-funding agency of the United Nations, with 193 member states.

Our mission is to lead the development of a balanced and effective international IP system that enables innovation and creativity for the benefit of all. Our mandate, governing bodies and procedures are set out in the WIPO Convention, which established WIPO in 1967.

Video: WIPO in three minutes

Quick facts: History: established in 1967 | Membership: 193 member states | Director General: Daren Tang | Headquarters: Geneva, Switzerland

Global Innovation Index (GII) (CONTD.,)

INDIA

40th India ranks 40th among the 132 economies featured in the GII 2022.

The Global Innovation Index (GII) ranks world economies according to their innovation capabilities. Consisting of roughly 80 indicators, grouped into innovation inputs and outputs, the GII aims to capture the multi-dimensional facets of innovation.

The following table shows the rankings of India over the past three years, noting that data availability and changes to the GII model framework influence year-on-year comparisons of the GII rankings. The statistical confidence interval for the ranking of India in the GII 2022 is between ranks 39 and 41.

Rankings for India (2020–2022)

GIIYR	GII	Innovation inputs	Innovation outputs
2020	48	57	45
2021	46	57	45
2022	40	42	39

Indoctrination is the arch-enemy of innovation

Global Competitiveness Index

World Economic Forum's Global Competitiveness Index: Ranks countries based on factors that contribute to their economic competitiveness and growth.

https://www.imd.org/centers/wcc/world-competitiveness-center/rankings/world-competitiveness-ranking/2023/#:~:text=IMD%20World%20Competitiveness%20Ranking%202023,the%20prosperity%20of%2064%20economies.

IMD World Competitiveness Ranking 2023
An overview

Released on 20 June 2023, the data explores multiple factors that affect the prosperity of 64 economies.

Agile governance and good access to markets boost citizens' quality of life, says new IMD research

IMD's World Competitiveness Center's latest report on global economic competitiveness gives leaders guidance for navigating a "fragmented" world.

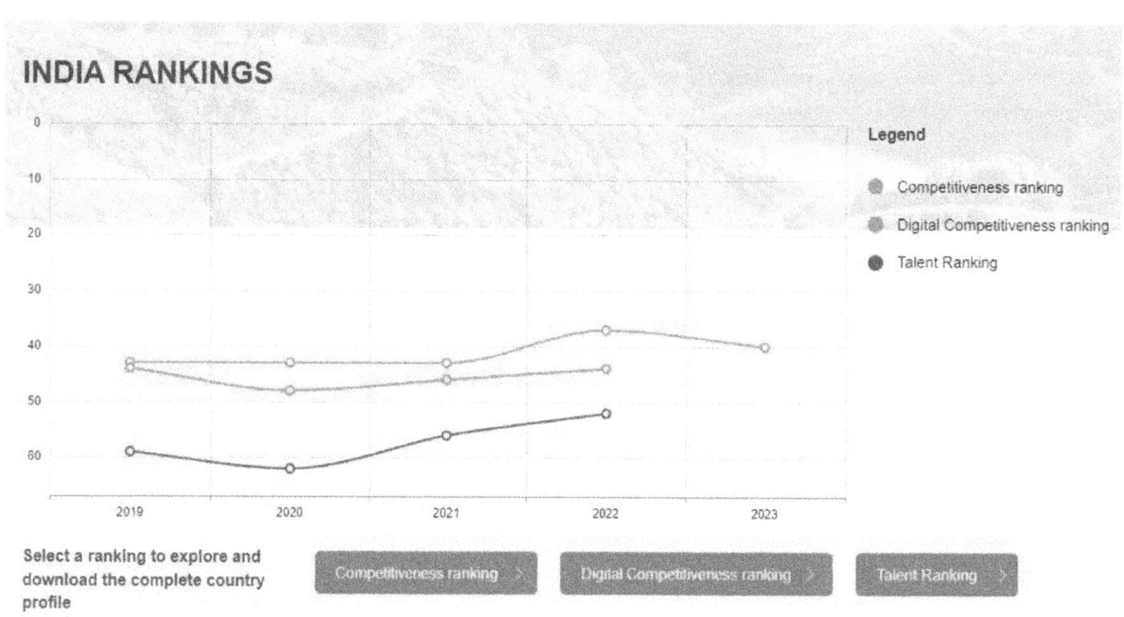

Competitiveness Ranking: 40
Digital Competitiveness Ranking: 44
Talent Ranking: 52

OECD Better Life Index

Allows users to compare well-being across countries based on various indicators like housing, income, jobs, community, education, environment, governance, health, life satisfaction, safety, and work-life balance.

https://www.oecdbetterlifeindex.org/

There is more to life than the cold numbers of GDP and economic statistics — This Index allows you to compare well-being across countries, based on 11 topics the OECD has identified as essential, in the areas of material living conditions and quality of life.

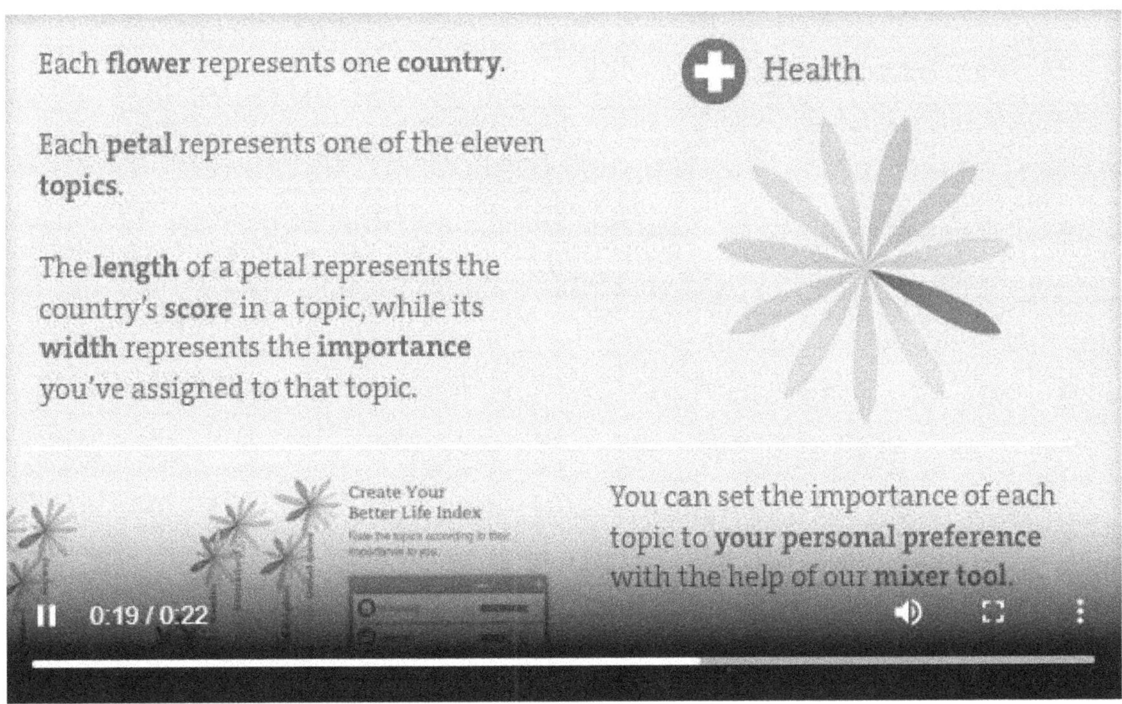

OECD Better Life Index (contd.,)

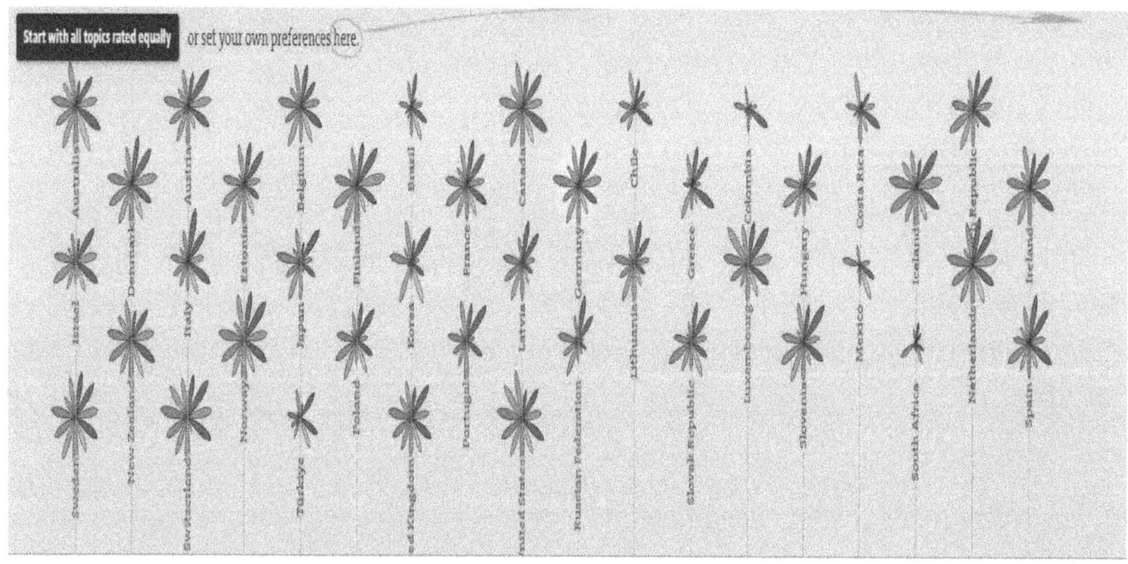

India is not one of the flowers displayed on the chart.

India is one of the many non-member economies with which the OECD has working relationships in addition to its member countries.The OECD has been co-operating with India since 1995.

Reflecting presence of huge market barriers in the country, India stood at 47th position in Services Trade Restrictiveness Index(STRI) conducted by the Organisation for Economic Cooperation and Development (OECD) for the year 2022.

Global Slavery Index

Estimates the prevalence of modern slavery in terms of human trafficking, forced labor, and other forms of exploitation.

About Global Slavery Index 2023

The fifth edition of the Global Slavery Index provides a global overview of modern slavery and is based on the 2022 estimates. The index is created by Walk Free, a human rights organization, and is based on data from the Global Estimates of Modern Slavery, produced by the International Labour Organization (ILO), Walk Free, and International Organization for Migration (IOM).

https://www.walkfree.org/global-slavery-index/

INDIA

PREVALENCE PER 1,000 PEOPLE: 8

VULNERABILITY OUT OF 100: 56

GOV RESPONSE OUT OF 100: 46

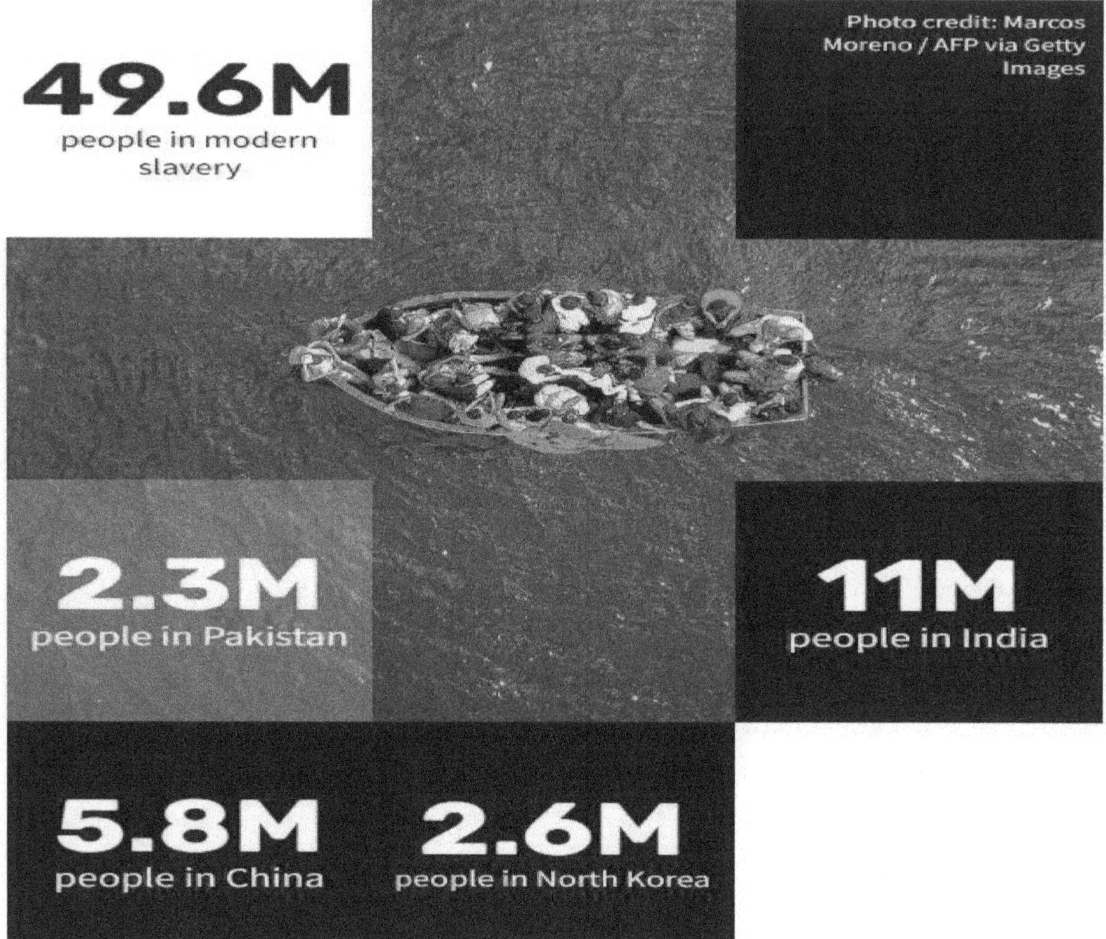

Strait of Gibraltar, Atlantic Ocean, September 2018. A boat carrying migrants is stranded at sea. Many migrants are driven to leave their homes due to conflict, or displacement caused by climate change.

An estimated 50 million people were living in modern slavery on any given day in 2021. This is nearly one in every 150 people in the world. Modern slavery is hidden in plain sight and is deeply intertwined with life in every corner of the world.

Global Terrorism Index (GTI) 2023
Measures the impact and trends of terrorism on a global scale.

The GTI report is produced by the Institute for Economics & Peace (IEP), a think tank, using data from Terrorism Tracker and other sources. Terrorism Tracker provides event records on terrorist attacks since 1 January 2007. The data set contains almost 66,000 terrorist incidents for the period 2007 to 2022.

This is the tenth edition of the Global Terrorism Index (GTI). This report provides a comprehensive summary of the key global trends and patterns in terrorism over the last decade. The calculation of the GTI score considers not only deaths but also incidents, hostages and injuries from terrorism, weighted over a five-year period.

India: Rank: 13 Score: 7.175

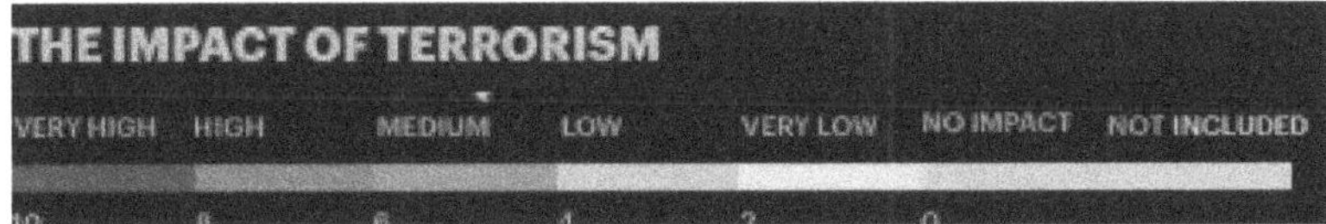

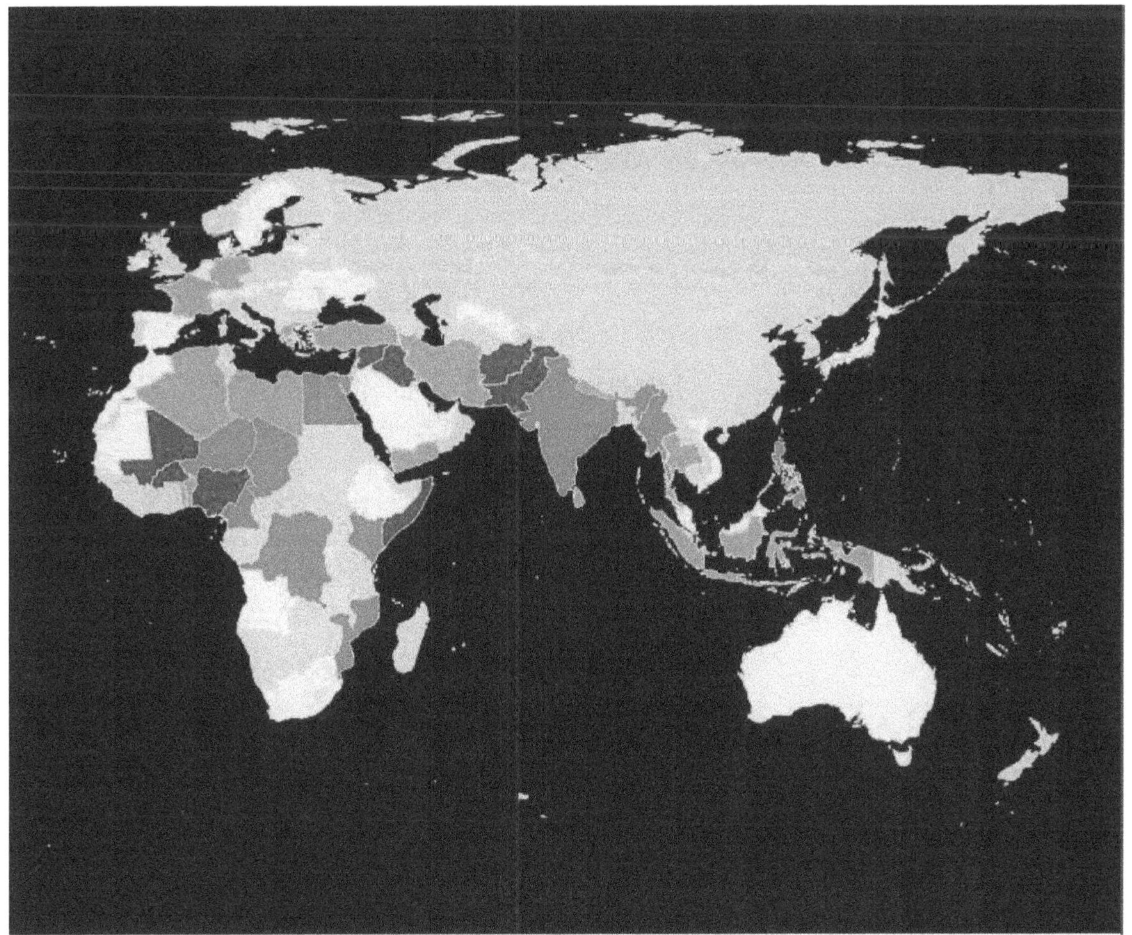

Global Soft Power Index 2023

India has been <u>ranked 28 </u>in Brand Finance's <u>Global Soft Power Index for 2023</u>.

Brand Finance index is based on a survey of 111,364 people across 101 countries.

<u>https://brandfinance.com/</u>

Governance Indicators

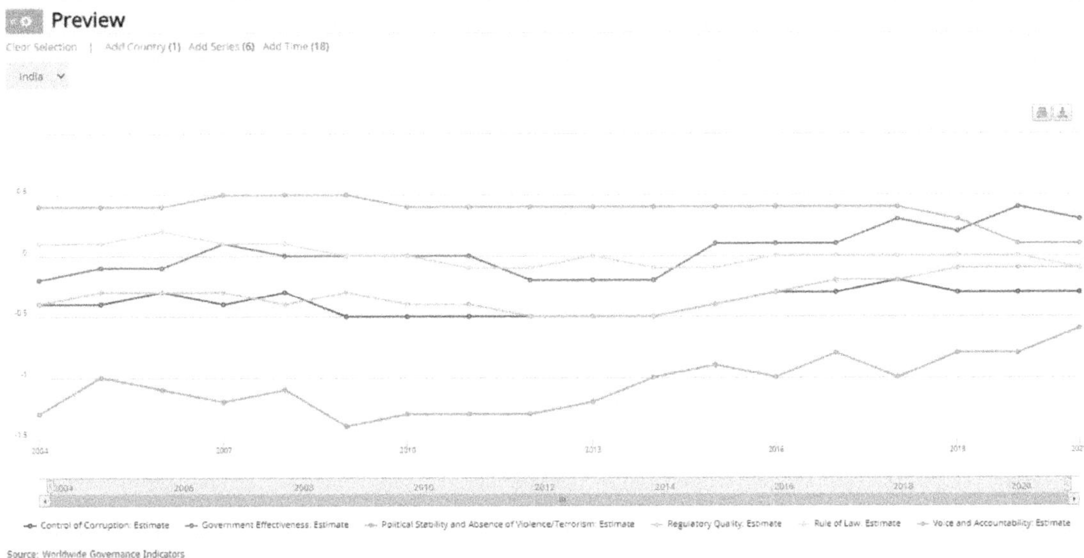

Click on the image and the click lens icon.

Exports of Goods and Services

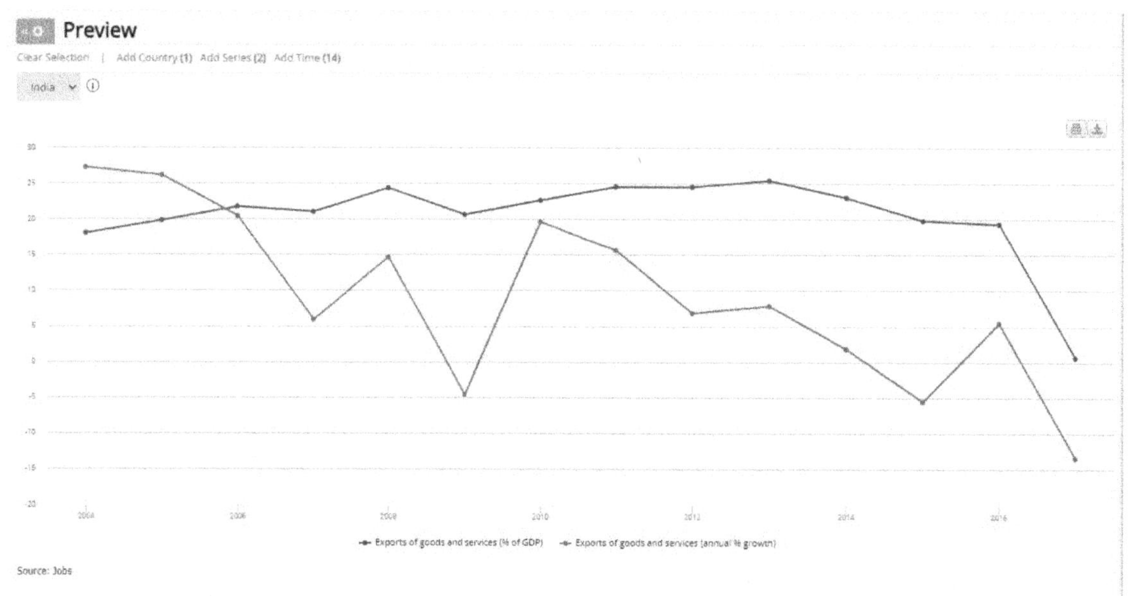

Exports of Goods and Services (% of GDP) fell from 25.14 in 2013 to **0.6** in 2016. (No data available after 2016)

Exports of Goods and Services (annual % growth) fell from 7.8 in 2013 to **-13.5** in 2016 (No data available after 2016)

It is puzzling.

Real Interest Rate

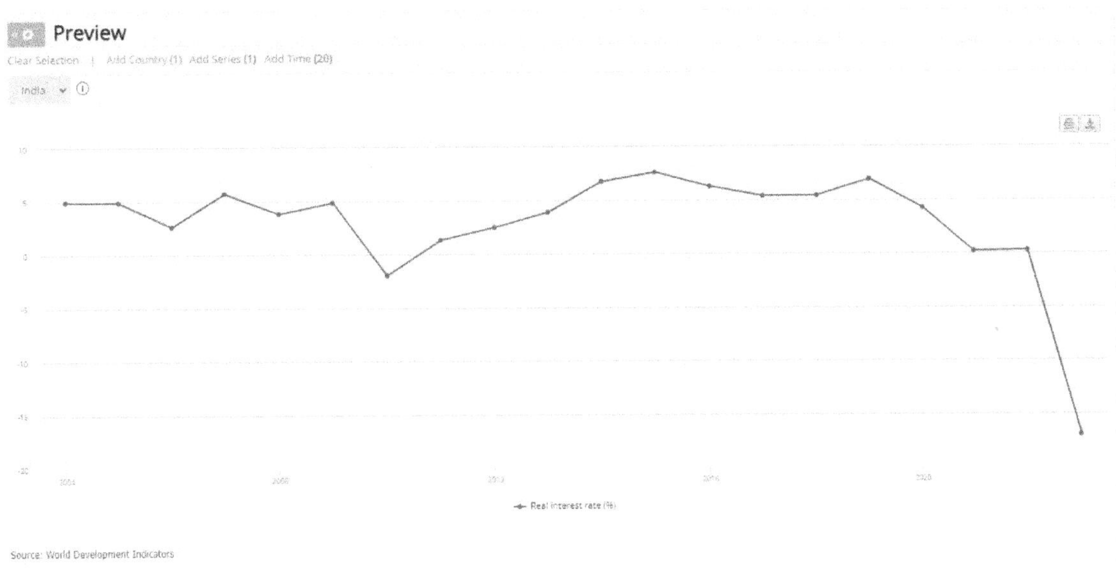

Sidebar

R*
The real (after inflation) interest rate that would prevail when the economy is operating at potential. Models of the macro-economy say monetary policy is delivering stimulus if and only if the prevailing real interest rate set by the central bank is lower than r*.

Real Effective Exchange Rate Index (2010 = 100)

Sidebar

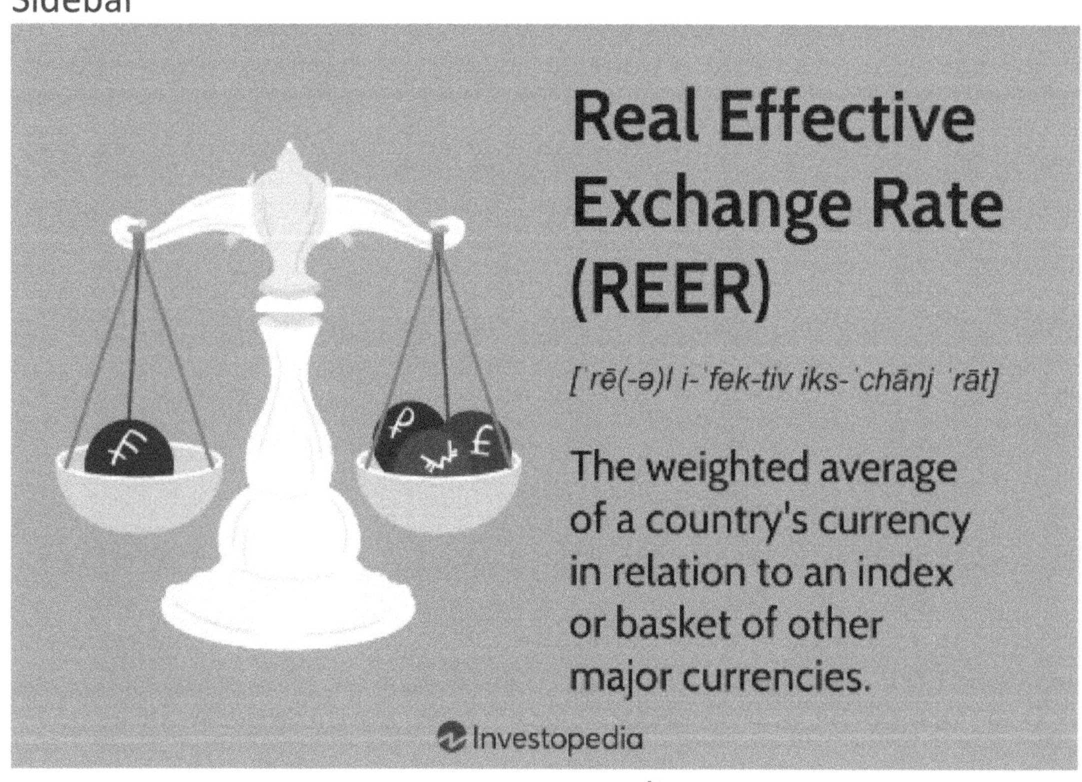

Appndix

The concepts of REER (Real Effective Exchange Rate) and trade competitiveness are both important in the context of international trade and economic analysis. Let's break down each concept:

Real Effective Exchange Rate (REER):

The exchange rate is the value of one country's currency in terms of another country's currency. The nominal exchange rate tells you how much of one currency you can get for a unit of another currency. However, this nominal exchange rate doesn't always provide an accurate representation of a country's international competitiveness because it doesn't account for differences in inflation rates between countries.
The Real Effective Exchange Rate (REER) is a measure that adjusts the nominal exchange rate for differences in inflation rates. It reflects the relative value of a country's currency against a basket of currencies of its trading partners, adjusted for price changes (inflation) in both domestic and partner countries. In simple terms, REER takes into account not only the nominal exchange rate but also the changes in price levels that affect the competitiveness of a country's goods and services in international markets.

If a country's REER appreciates (increases), it means that its currency has become relatively stronger compared to its trading partners' currencies. This can make its exports more expensive for other countries and imports cheaper for its own citizens, potentially affecting trade balances.

Trade Competitiveness:
Trade competitiveness refers to a country's ability to sell its goods and services in international markets successfully. It is influenced by a variety of factors, including:

Price Competitiveness: This is closely related to the REER. If a country's currency appreciates significantly, its goods and services become more expensive for foreign buyers, potentially leading to a decrease in exports.

Quality and Innovation: The quality of a country's products and its ability to innovate can greatly impact its competitiveness in global markets. High-quality and innovative products are often in demand regardless of exchange rate fluctuations.

Productivity: Higher productivity allows a country to produce goods and services more efficiently, which can lead to cost savings and better prices for consumers.

Infrastructure and Logistics: Efficient infrastructure and logistics networks can reduce the costs of transporting goods, making a country's exports more competitive.

Regulations and Business Environment: A favorable business environment, including supportive regulations and ease of doing business, can attract both domestic and foreign investment, enhancing a country's trade competitiveness.

Human Capital: A skilled and educated workforce can contribute to the production of high-value goods and services, boosting a country's competitiveness.

In summary, the REER is a measure that takes into account both nominal exchange rates and inflation differentials to assess a country's currency's relative value. Trade competitiveness, on the other hand, encompasses a broader range of factors that influence a country's ability to effectively participate in international trade. Both concepts are crucial for understanding a country's trade dynamics and economic performance in the global marketplace.

The concepts of REER (Real Effective Exchange Rate) and trade competitiveness are both important in the context of international trade and economic analysis. Let's break down each concept:

Real Effective Exchange Rate (REER):
The exchange rate is the value of one country's currency in terms of another country's currency. The nominal exchange rate tells you how much of one currency you can get for a unit of another currency. However, this nominal exchange rate doesn't always provide an accurate representation of a country's international competitiveness because it doesn't account for differences in inflation rates between countries.
The Real Effective Exchange Rate (REER) is a measure that adjusts the nominal exchange rate for differences in inflation rates. It reflects the relative value of a country's currency against a basket of currencies of its trading partners, adjusted for price changes (inflation) in both domestic and partner countries. In simple terms, REER takes into account not only the nominal exchange rate but also the changes in price levels that affect the competitiveness of a country's goods and services in international markets.

If a country's REER appreciates (increases), it means that its currency has become relatively stronger compared to its trading partners' currencies. This can make its exports more expensive for other countries and imports cheaper for its own citizens, potentially affecting trade balances.

Trade Competitiveness:

Trade competitiveness refers to a country's ability to sell its goods and services in international markets successfully. It is influenced by a variety of factors, including:

Price Competitiveness: This is closely related to the REER. If a country's currency appreciates significantly, its goods and services become more expensive for foreign buyers, potentially leading to a decrease in exports.

Quality and Innovation: The quality of a country's products and its ability to innovate can greatly impact its competitiveness in global markets. High-quality and innovative products are often in demand regardless of exchange rate fluctuations.

Productivity: Higher productivity allows a country to produce goods and services more efficiently, which can lead to cost savings and better prices for consumers.

Infrastructure and Logistics: Efficient infrastructure and logistics networks can reduce the costs of transporting goods, making a country's exports more competitive.

Regulations and Business Environment: A favorable business environment, including supportive regulations and ease of doing business, can attract both domestic and foreign investment, enhancing a country's trade competitiveness.

Human Capital: A skilled and educated workforce can contribute to the production of high-value goods and services, boosting a country's competitiveness.

In summary, the REER is a measure that takes into account both nominal exchange rates and inflation differentials to assess a country's currency's relative value. Trade competitiveness, on the other hand, encompasses a broader range of factors that influence a country's ability to effectively participate in international trade. Both concepts are crucial for understanding a country's trade dynamics and economic performance in the global marketplace.

User

Is there a global trade competitive index? If so, what is India's rank?

ChatGPT

As of my last knowledge update in September 2021, there are several global indices that attempt to measure trade competitiveness and overall economic competitiveness. One of the prominent indices is the World Economic Forum's "Global Competitiveness Index" which assesses a country's overall competitiveness based on a wide range of factors including infrastructure, macroeconomic stability, health, education, innovation, and more. However, it's important to note that these indices might not exclusively focus on trade competitiveness.

For more specific trade competitiveness rankings, the "World Competitiveness Ranking" by the International Institute for Management Development (IMD) is one of the well-known indices. Another important index is the "Ease of Doing Business" ranking by the World Bank, which assesses various factors affecting business operations, including trade-related measures.

It's possible that there have been updates or changes to these indices since September 2021. To get the most accurate and up-to-date information on India's trade competitiveness rank, I recommend checking the latest reports and publications from reputable sources such as the World Economic Forum, IMD, and the World Bank.

User

I did research Ease of doing business. I want to know how strongly the two are correlated.

ChatGPT

The ease of doing business and trade competitiveness are related concepts, but they focus on slightly different aspects of a country's economic environment. While there can be correlations between the two, they don't necessarily have a direct one-to-one relationship. Let's explore how they are correlated and how they differ:

Correlation between Ease of Doing Business and Trade Competitiveness:

Both ease of doing business and trade competitiveness are influenced by factors such as regulatory environment, infrastructure, administrative efficiency, and the overall business climate. Countries that rank well in terms of ease of doing business often have streamlined regulations, efficient customs procedures, and supportive infrastructure, which can contribute to their trade competitiveness. For example, a country with simplified customs procedures, efficient logistics networks, and minimal bureaucratic hurdles might be more attractive for international trade, potentially leading to higher trade competitiveness.

Differences between Ease of Doing Business and Trade Competitiveness:

While there is overlap between the two concepts, they have different scopes. Ease of doing business primarily focuses on the regulatory environment for businesses operating within a country. It measures factors such as starting a business, dealing with construction permits, getting electricity, registering property, getting credit, protecting minority investors, paying taxes, trading across borders, enforcing contracts, and resolving insolvency. These factors collectively impact the overall business environment.

Trade competitiveness, on the other hand, takes into account a broader set of factors that influence a country's ability to compete in international markets. This includes factors like the quality and innovation of products, the country's export-import ratio, trade balances, currency exchange rates, tariff structures, and non-tariff barriers to trade. Trade competitiveness is more directly tied to a country's ability to sell its goods and services abroad and its overall performance in global markets.

In summary, while there is likely a correlation between ease of doing business and trade competitiveness, they assess different aspects of a country's economic environment. A favorable business climate can contribute to trade competitiveness, but other factors like innovation, product quality, and macroeconomic conditions also play significant roles in determining a country's success in global trade.

User

I was hoping for a regression coefficient and equation. Thank you very much for the pointers.

ChatGPT

I apologize for any confusion, but providing a specific regression coefficient and equation between ease of doing business and trade competitiveness isn't possible without access to the latest and most comprehensive data. Moreover, such a coefficient would depend on the specific variables and data sources used in the analysis.

If you're interested in exploring the correlation between ease of doing business and trade competitiveness for a specific country or set of countries, you would need to gather relevant data on both ease of doing business scores and trade competitiveness rankings for those countries. Once you have the data, you can perform a statistical analysis, potentially including regression analysis, to determine the degree of correlation between these variables.

When conducting such an analysis, you would typically compare the ease of doing business scores with trade competitiveness indicators (such as export performance, trade balances, etc.) to see how closely they are related. However, it's important to note that correlation does not imply causation, and there could be other factors influencing both variables.

To get accurate and up-to-date results, I recommend consulting economic research, academic papers, and reports from reputable international organizations such as the World Bank, the World Economic Forum, and other research institutions that specialize in economic analysis and trade studies.

The IMD World Competitiveness Ranking

INDIA RANKINGS

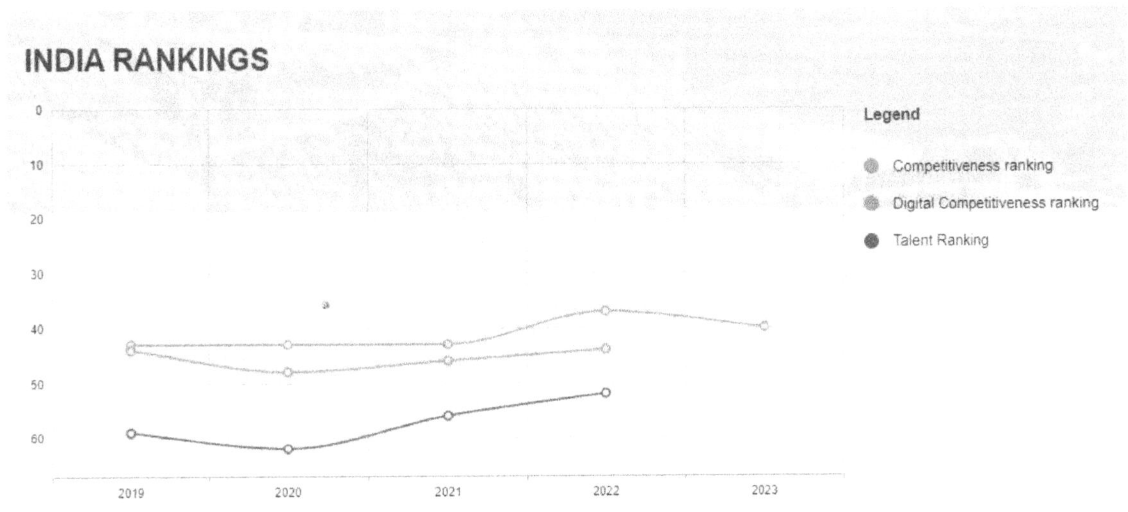

https://worldcompetitiveness.imd.org/countryprofile/overview/IN

Table 5.5. Trends in Nominal and Real Effective Exchange Rate of Rupee				
(Trade Based Weights)				
Year/month (Average)	Nominal effective exchange rate (NEER) 6-currency Index	Real effective exchange rate (REER) 6-Currency Index	Nominal effective exchange rate (NEER) 36-currency Index	Real effective exchange rate (REER) 36-Curreney Index
(1)	(2)	(3)	(4)	(5)
Base Year: 1993-94=100				
1994-95	96.86	105.71	99.21	104.59
1995-96	88.45	101.14	91.65	98.42
1996-97	86.73	100.97	89.08	96.64
1997-98	87.80	104.24	92.17	100.95
1998-99	77.37	95.99	88.76	92.84
1999-00	77.03	97.52	90.90	95.75
2000-01	77.30	102.65	92.11	100.04
2001-02	75.89	102.49	91.52	100.87
2002-03	71.09	97.43	89.22	98.19
2003-04	69.75	98.85	87.15	99.50
2004-05	69.26	101.35	87.28	100.05
Base Year: 2004-05=100				
2005-06	103.04	104.45	102.24	102.38
2006-07	98.09	103.82	97.63	100.76
2007-08	104.62	113.44	104.75	109.20
2008-09	90.42	103.94	93.34	99.65
2009-10	87.07	110.73	90.94	103.88
2010-11	91.83	124.50	93.54	112.68
2011-12	84.44	121.17	87.38	110.27
2012-13	75.59	117.15	78.32	105.57
2013-14	67.76	112.80	72.32	103.27
2014-15	68.60	119.92	74.07	108.96
2015-16	67.52	122.71	74.75	112.08
2016-17	66.86	125.17	74.65	114.51
2017-18	67.91	129.19	76.94	119.71
2018-19	63.07	121.70	72.64	114.01
2019-20	63.59	125.76	73.28	116.75

Table 5.5. Trends in Nominal and Real Effective Exchange Rate of Rupee

(Trade Based Weights)

Year/month (Average)	Nominal effective exchange rate (NEER) 6-currency Index	Real effective exchange rate (REER) 6-Currency Index	Nominal effective exchange rate (NEER) 40-currency Index	Real effective exchange rate (REER) 40-Currency Index
(1)	(2)	(3)	(4)	(5)
Base Year: 2015-16=100				
2004-05	139.77	75.30	133.77	89.21
2005-06	145.23	79.94	136.78	91.35
2006-07	139.62	80.45	130.61	89.89
2007-08	150.34	89.04	140.13	97.42
2008-09	130.86	82.26	124.86	88.90
2009-10	126.61	88.08	121.65	92.68
2010-11	134.55	100.43	125.13	100.53
2011-12	124.07	97.81	116.89	98.38
2012-13	111.26	94.73	104.77	94.19
2013-14	99.68	91.11	96.75	92.13
2014-15	101.08	97.09	99.09	97.21
2015-16	100.00	100.00	100.00	100.00
2016-17	99.48	102.63	100.08	101.80
2017-18	101.46	106.52	103.24	105.94
2018-19	94.19	100.29	97.45	100.63
2019-20	94.87	103.56	98.00	103.20
2020-21	88.45	101.84	93.92	103.46
2021-22	87.03	102.27	93.13	104.66
2022-23 (P)				
April	87.59	103.22	93.33	103.46
May	88.04	104.20	93.34	104.75
June	87.40	103.32	92.62	104.01
July	86.88	102.96	92.07	103.53
August	87.24	103.74	92.27	103.79
September	88.27	105.05	93.06	104.69
October	86.92	103.58	91.89	103.69
November	86.33	102.82	91.70	103.11
December	83.71	99.71	88.94	99.30

Source: Reserve Bank of India   P: Provisional

Notes 1: REER figures for the period 1994-95 to 2004-05 are based on Wholesale Price Index (WPI).

Notes 2: REER figures for the period 2005-06 to 2019-20 are based on Consumer Price Index (CPI).

SDG Atlas 2023

https://datatopics.worldbank.org/sdgatlas

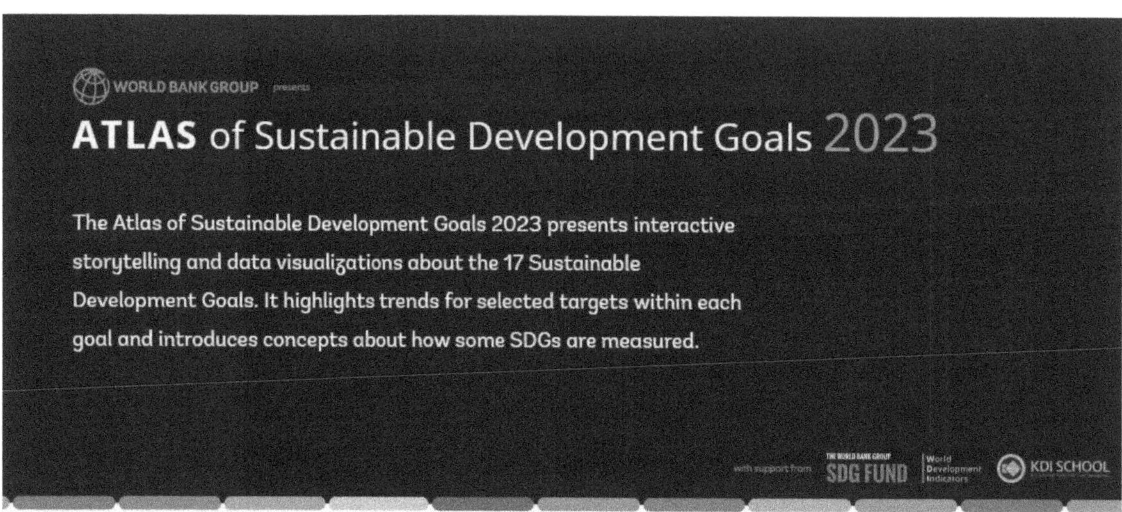

Explore stories for the 17 SDGs

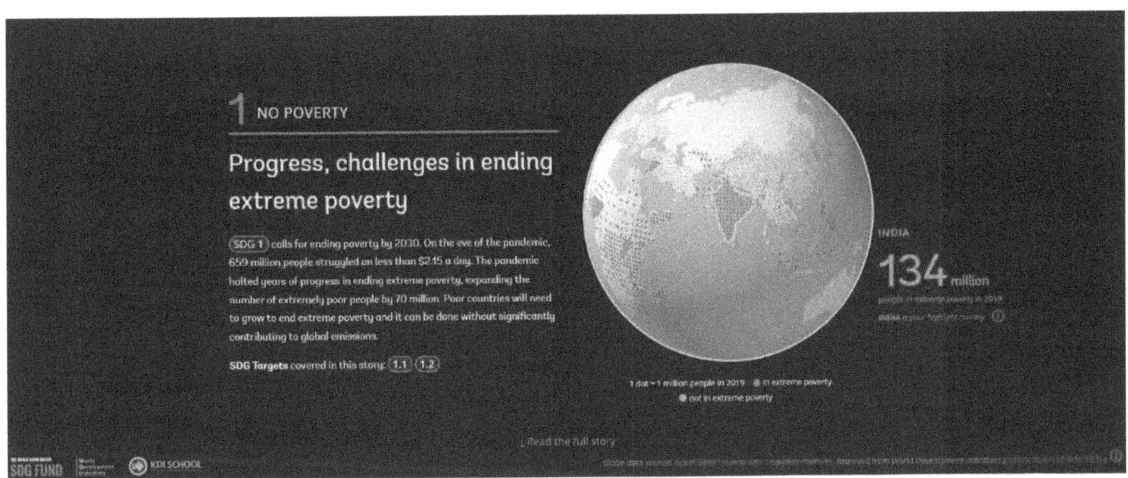

SDG target 1.1 aims to end extreme poverty everywhere by 2030. Individuals live in extreme poverty if their daily income or consumption is below the international poverty line, currently set at $2.15 per day. Over the past decades, the world has made significant progress in ending extreme poverty.

https://datatopics.worldbank.org/sdgatlas/goal-1-no-poverty#c1s4

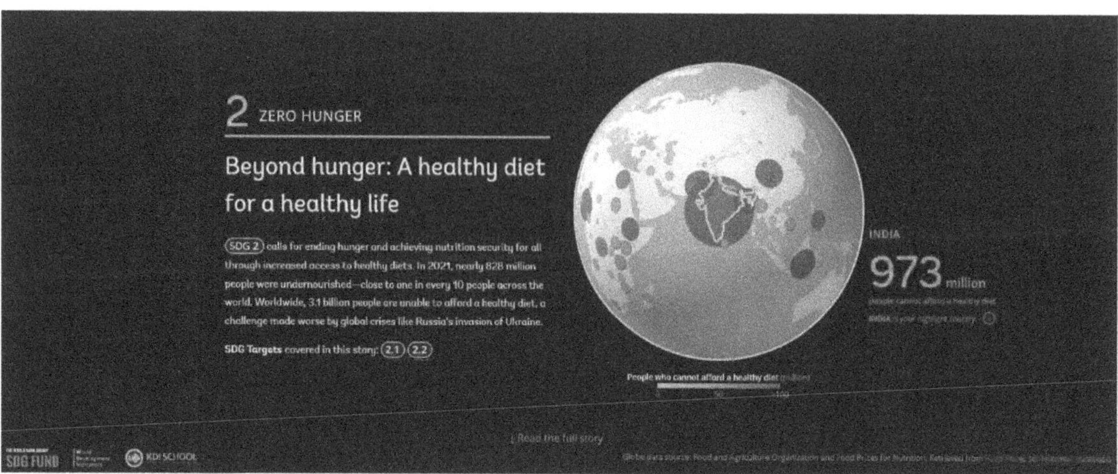

To sustain an active and healthy life, a person requires a balanced diet with sufficient calories, and an optimal balance of essential nutrients and food groups.

Many people around the world cannot afford enough food to meet their daily energy needs, and for others, healthy diets are too expensive. Food takes a sizable share of their income, leaving them with difficult choices.
Low food intake and unbalanced diets can lead to different forms of child malnutrition (ages 0 to 5) such as stunting, wasting, micronutrient deficiencies, being overweight and obesity, or a combination of those conditions SDG target 2.2. This often leads to adverse health consequences, poor developmental and learning outcomes, as well as lost economic productivity later in life.

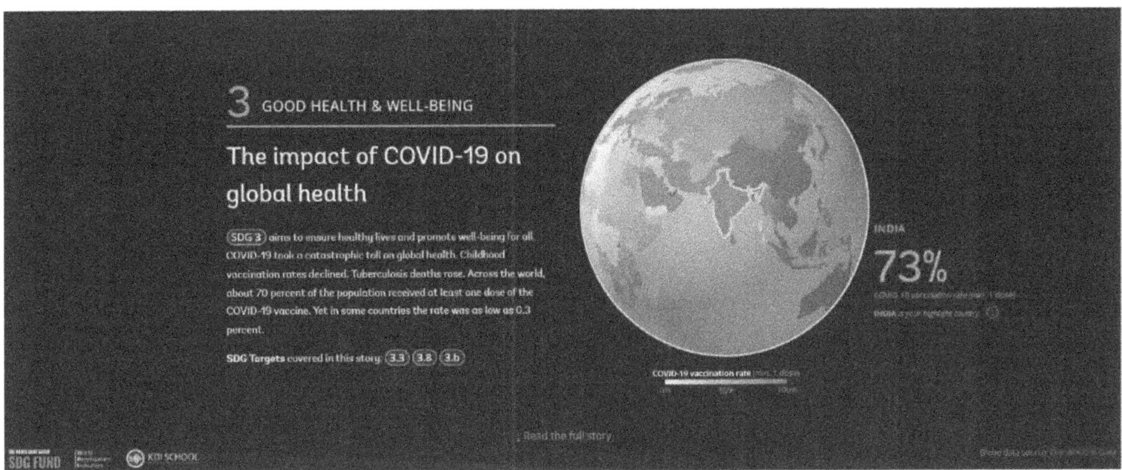

Millions of people worldwide died due to COVID-19. In addition to the lives lost from the virus, the pandemic made access to healthcare more difficult, especially in the first years and led to additional preventable deaths caused by other illnesses. Essential childhood vaccination rates also decreased, as did diagnosis rates for tuberculosis and access to malaria treatments.

The catastrophic death toll from COVID-19 does not tell the whole story. Studies indicate that, in addition to the fatalities reported by governments and attributed to COVID-19, many more people died in the first two years of the pandemic (2020 and 2021) compared with levels expected based on historical trends.

The true number of lives lost from COVID-19 may never be known because of difficulties in determining the cause of many deaths and in collecting accurate data.

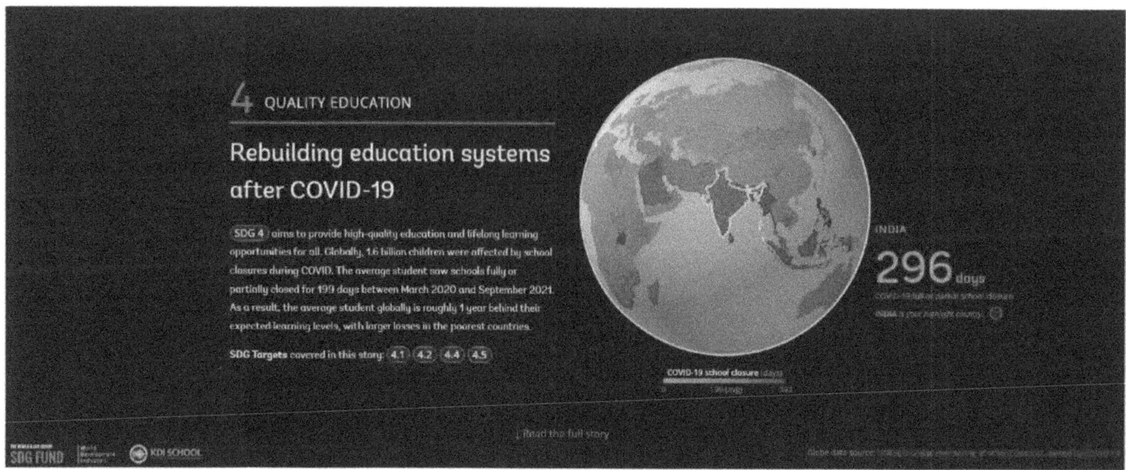

Prior to the COVID-19 pandemic, most countries were not on track to provide high-quality education to all children by 2030. Over half of children in low- and middle-income countries experienced learning poverty, meaning they were unable to understand a simple written text by the end of primary school. This indicator helps inform SDG target 4.1 as it captures both schooling and learning, combining the rate of children out of school (schooling) with the percentage who are in school but have not achieved basic reading proficiency (learning).

An Education Crisis
A country's income level is strongly related to learning poverty. Since COVID-19, learning poverty rates are estimated to have increased, and disparities between countries have widened.

Disparities in access to learning persist.

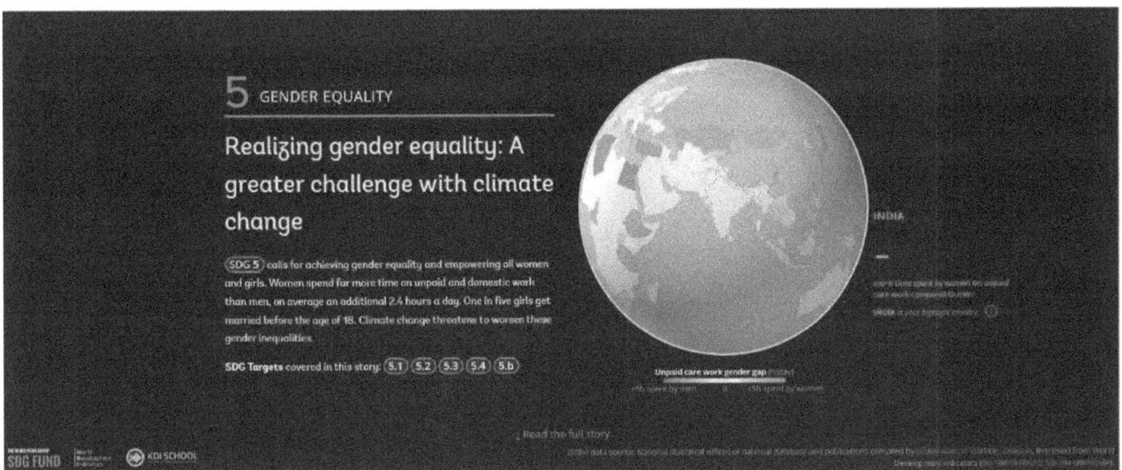

Gender driven inequalities are rooted in societal norms and systems. Women generally experience limited agency or decision-making power, restricted mobility, and limited access to financial resources. They face numerous challenges, including child marriage, domestic violence, and the burden of unpaid domestic work as well as responsibilities related to child and elder care. Also, women, on average, enjoy only three-fourths of the legal rights pertaining to economic opportunities that men possess.SDG target 5.1

With climate change SDG 13, the challenges will intensify. Although climate change affects all segments of society, its impact can vary, often exacerbating existing inequalities. Gender disparities that already exist can hinder women's capacity to adapt to weather-related disturbances. Moreover, as weather events become more frequent and severe, gender inequalities have the potential to not only persist but also escalate.

The first example below reports existing gender inequalities in domestic work and shows how climate change is making things worse.

Gendered roles in the household
Within households, there is often a division of tasks between women and men. This division arises from cultural norms that assign men the role of primary breadwinners, while women are expected to fulfill the primary caregiving responsibilities. Consequently, worldwide, women bear the majority of the burden when it comes to domestic and unpaid care work.SDG target 5.4

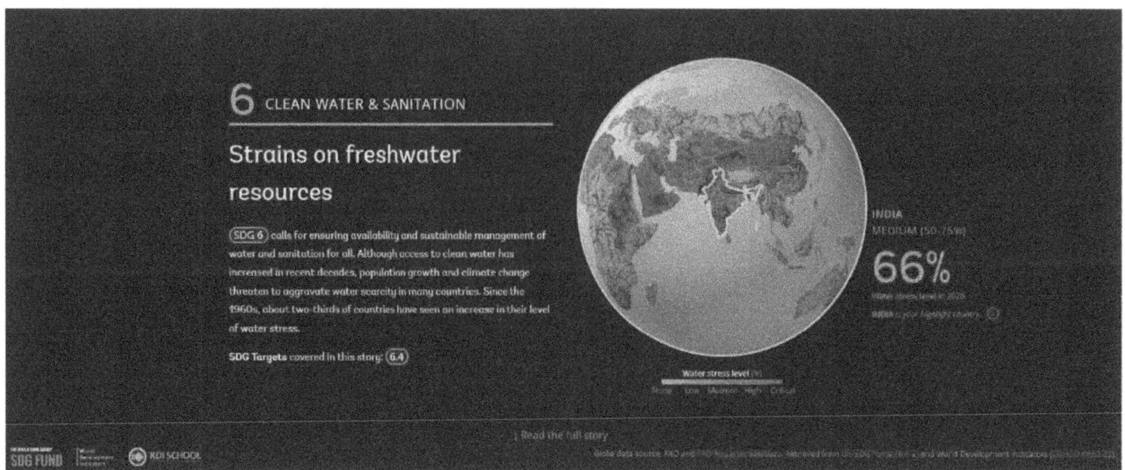

Over the past twenty years, global access to water has steadily increased. Close to three quarters of the world population used safely managed drinking water services SDG target 6.1 in 2020, up from 62 percent in 2000. However this progress is threatened by increasing demand for freshwater, and the impact of climate change on the water cycle.

This chapter will focus on SDG target 6.4, which seeks to ensure sustainable usage and supply of freshwater, and avert water scarcity.

Freshwater is a limited resource

Looking at the Earth, water may seem abundant. But freshwater, non-saline water that can be used for irrigation and consumed by humans, is limited. Freshwater represents only 2.5 percent of the total amount of water available on the planet.

Easily accessible surface freshwater accounts for less than 1% of the total
Water distribution on Earth (% of total water)

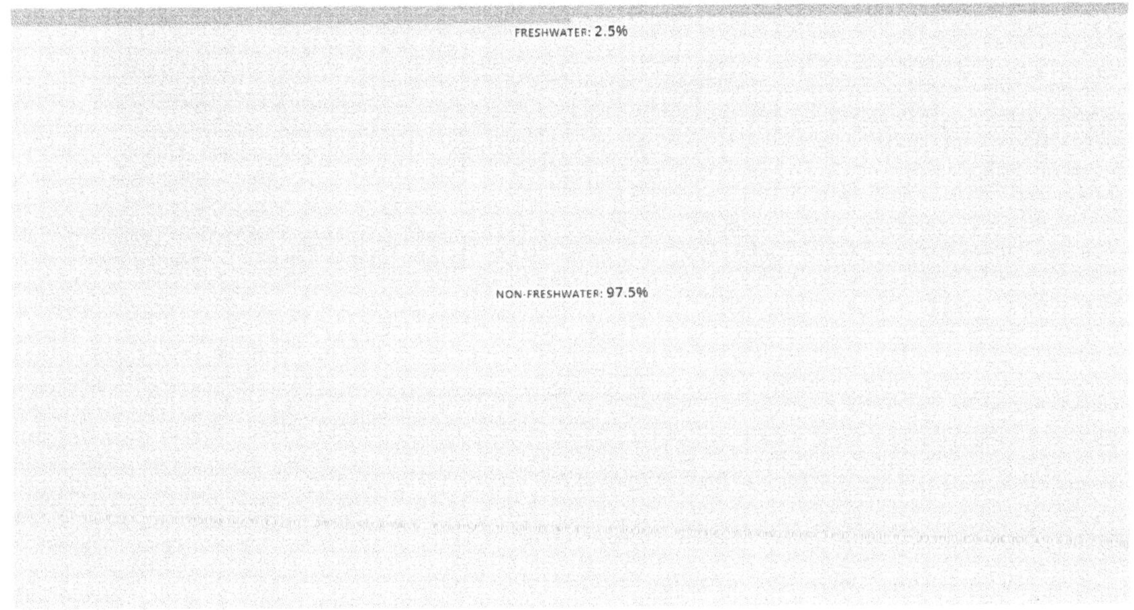

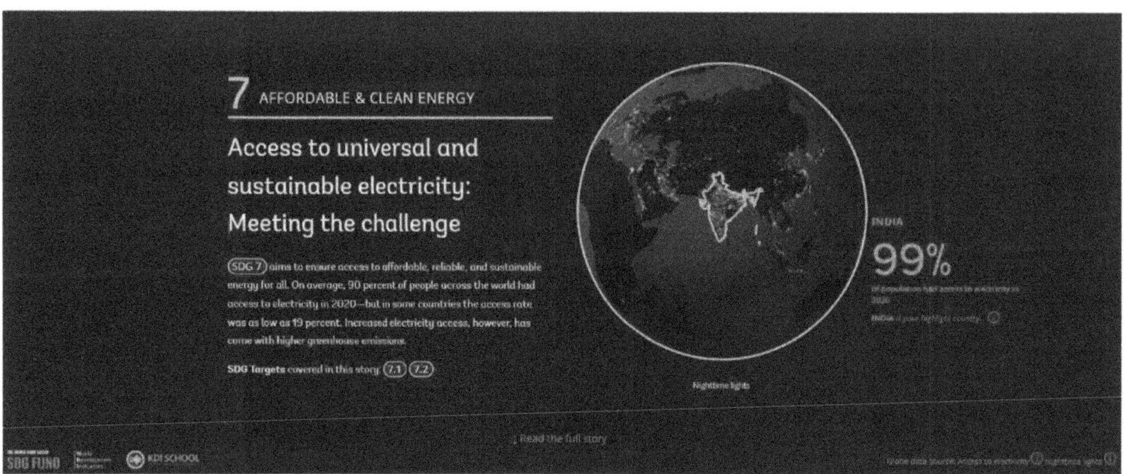

Under SDG 7, countries face the often conflicting challenge of bringing electricity
to all, SDG target 7.1, and at the same time increasing the proportion generated
using renewable sources to reduce greenhouse gas emissions, SDG target 7.2.
Both targets must be addressed simultaneously by 2030.

Global access to electricity is increasing at a slow pace
Progress towards achieving universal access to electricity (SDG indicator 7.1.1) has
been slow over the last 20 years. The share of the global population with access
to electricity increased from 78 percent in 2000 to 91 percent in 2020. Based on
current trends, this figure is expected to rise only marginally from 91 percent in
2020 to 92 percent by 2030.

Visualizing access to electricity through nighttime lights
One way to visualize access to electricity is through nighttime lights captured by
satellite images. This can be a useful complementary tool to fill the gaps from
household survey data, the typical source for measuring electricity access,
collected once every few years.

In cases in which surveys cannot be conducted, such as in conflict areas, nighttime
lights are especially useful to get an approximation of an area' s electricity usage.
It is worth noting that nighttime lights primarily capture public or street lighting
and likely miss rural households that access electricity through off-grid
technologies.Despite its large population, a single region stands out for having the
fewest lights visible at nighttime: Sub-Saharan Africa. Nighttime lights can help
visualize the current state of electrification in this region.

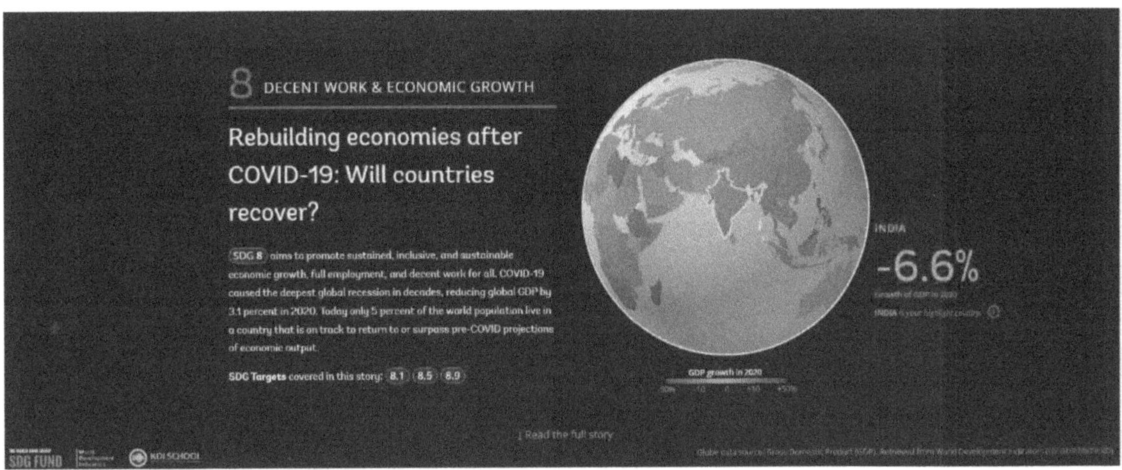

The global emergence of COVID-19 in 2020 SDG target 3.3, along with the accompanying government measures taken to contain the disease, caused the greatest reduction in global economic activity since World War II SDG target 8.1. Following this shock and others such as inflation and Russia' s invasion of Ukraine, the world is not on track to make up the lost economic output in the foreseeable future.

The damage done
Global GDP growth
-3.1%
IN 2020

The global economy had been growing at a steady pace since 2010, but this trend abruptly reversed in 2020. It was the worst economic decline in decades. Gross Domestic Product (GDP) dropped 3.1 percent in 2020 – more than twice the contraction seen in 2009 following the global financial crisis.

Only 23 countries out of 188 are on track to recover from COVID-19 impacts by 2023

India and Indonesia, two of the most populated countries in the world, have both taken a major economic hit. In 2023, India's GDP is expected to see a shortfall of around $296 billion compared to pre-COVID expectations, 8.7 percent below earlier projections. Indonesia's GDP will be around $107 billion lower, 8.3 percent below the 2020 projection, and both countrys' economy is not expected to make up the lost ground at least through 2025. This suggests long-lasting damage.

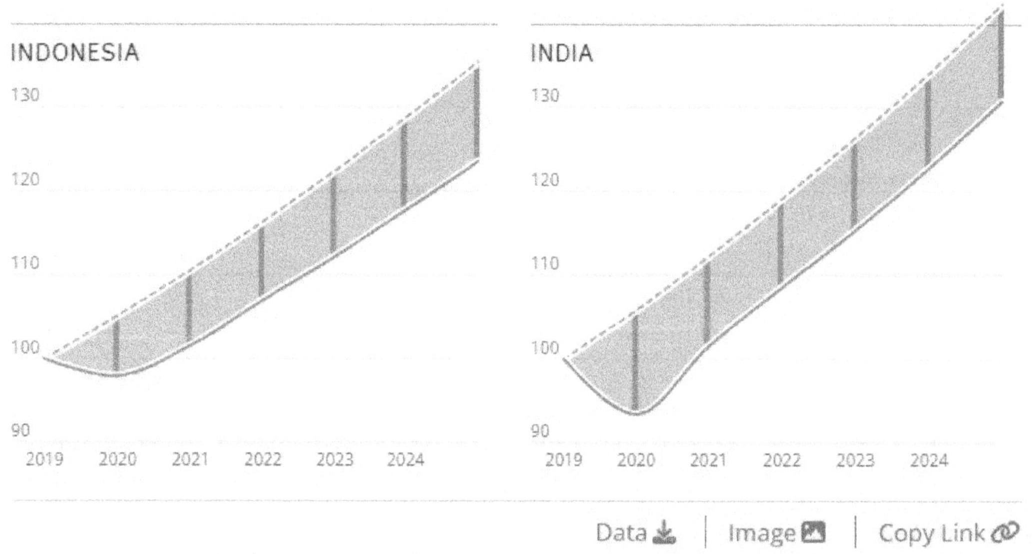

Growth in India and Indonesia not on track to make up lost GDP

Level of GDP compared to pre-COVID projections (value for 2019=100)

Source: Global Economic Prospects (NYGDPMKTPKDZ). World Development Indicators (NY.GDP.MKTP.KD).

https://datatopics.worldbank.org/sdgatlas/goal-8-decent-work-and-economic-growth#c17

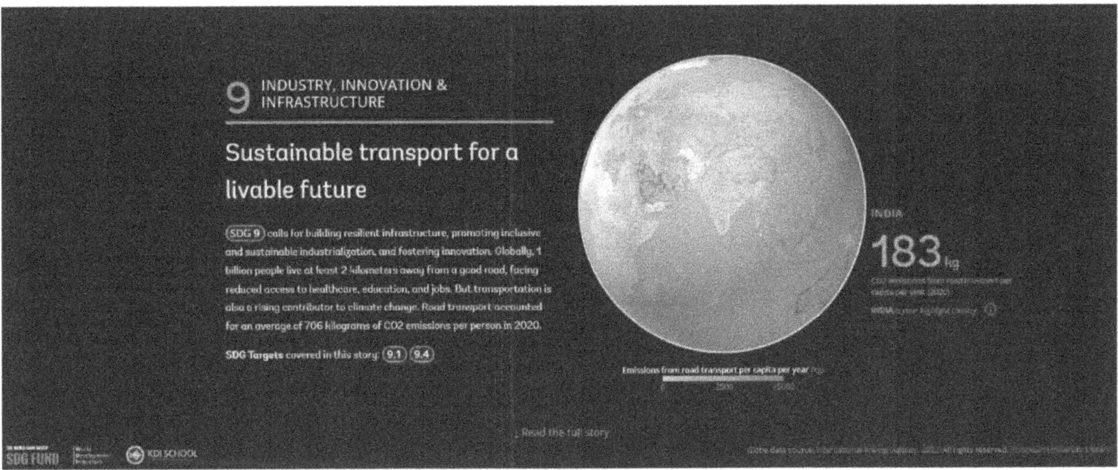

Transportation is essential for ensuring access to better economic, health and education opportunities. One of the targets of SDG 9 is to expand the availability of reliable infrastructure, including transport, that can support human and economic development. SDG target 9.1

Transportation (by road, air, sea) is also a major source of greenhouse gas emissions and hence a contributor to climate change. The transportation sector accounts for a quarter of global CO2 emissions. Countries face the challenge of expanding access to transport so that it is sustainable and clean.

Transport is essential for human development

Many people in low-income countries, particularly in rural areas, do not have access to roads or reliable transportation. One way to determine the level of access to reliable infrastructure SDG target 9.1, is the Rural Access Index (RAI) (SDG indicator 9.1.1), which measures the share of the rural population in a specific country or region living within 2 km of an all-season road. Globally, an estimated one billion people lack such access, representing one in eight people in the world.

In Sub-Saharan Africa, where almost 60 percent of the population lives outside urban areas, RAI scores can range from 17 percent of the rural population in Zambia (2011) to 56 percent in Kenya (2009).

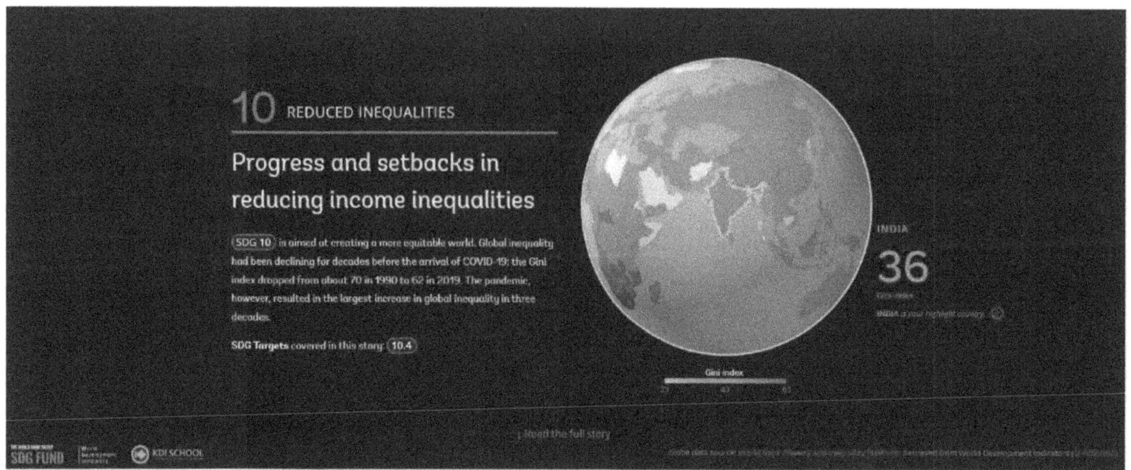

SDG 10 calls for reducing inequalities from several perspectives. This story will focus on income inequality as measured by the Gini index, an indicator of SDG target 10.4 .

Gini indices measure inequality on a scale from zero, indicating perfect equality, to 100, indicating one person having all resources. Countries' income Ginis typically lie within a range of 25 to 60.

The lowest Gini currently observed is 23 in Slovakia, while the highest is 63 in South Africa.

The global Gini
62
IN 2019

Ginis can also be calculated globally. The global Gini pools all people of the world together, adjusts their incomes for differences in purchasing power, and evaluates how far their incomes are from each other. This accounts for inequality within and among countries.

Inequality within countries concerns the degree to which individuals' incomes in a country differ from each other while inequality between countries concerns the degree to which countries' average incomes differ from each other. In Malawi, for example, average consumption in 2019 was less than $1,000 compared to more than $30,000 in the United States.

Because of the large differences in average incomes between countries, the global Gini tends to be higher than those in individual countries. In 2019, the global Gini was 62.

Global inequality declined until 2020 at which point the pandemic reversed the trend.

https://datatopics.worldbank.org/sdgatlas/goal-11-sustainable-cities-and-communities#c3s3

Municipal solid waste (referred to as waste hereafter) is a byproduct of material consumption. Uncollected or poorly managed waste leads to unhygienic conditions in communities and can severely impact people's health.

SDG 3 Managing waste is important for the environment also because it is a significant contributor to greenhouse gas emissions SDG 13 and can cause land SDG 15 and water pollution.

SDG 14

For cities to meet the SDG target 11.6 of avoiding adverse health and environmental impacts, waste must be collected and managed properly. In 2020, about 2.2 billion tonnes of waste was produced across the world.

This is equivalent to 376 kg of waste per capita or six times the weight of an average person.

India
189,750,000 Tonnes/per year
Waste generation per capita: 145 Tonnes/per year (in 2020)

The Changing Wealth of Nations

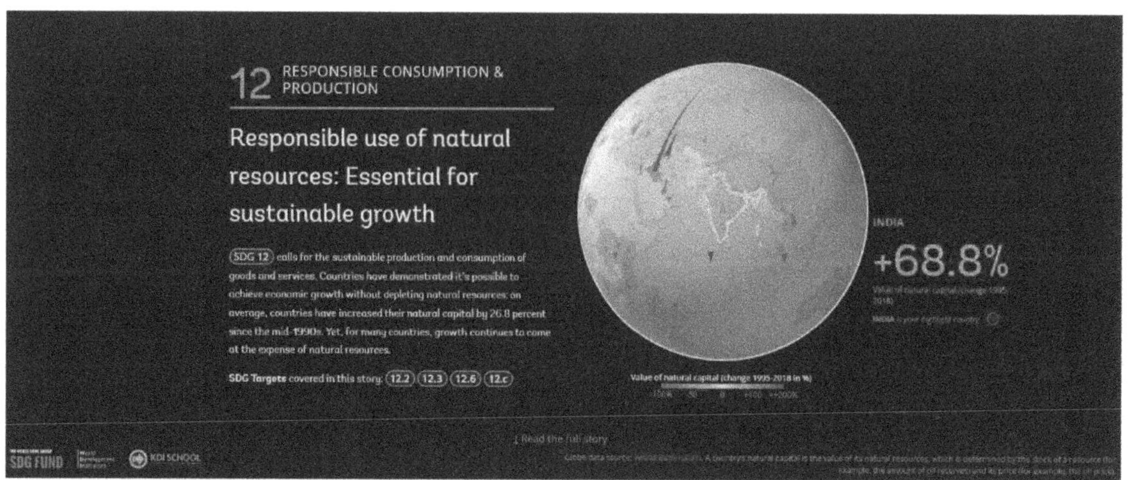

https://datatopics.worldbank.org/sdgatlas/goal-12-responsible-consumption-and-production

To assess the sustainability of a country's economy, we look at whether its income – Gross Domestic Product (GDP) – is generated by draining natural resources. This can be done using data from the Changing Wealth of Nations, a World Bank initiative.

According to the Changing Wealth of Nations, the wealth associated with a country's natural resources is determined by the stock of a resource (for example, the amount of oil reserves) and its price (for example, the oil price). The value of a country's natural resources is called its natural capital.

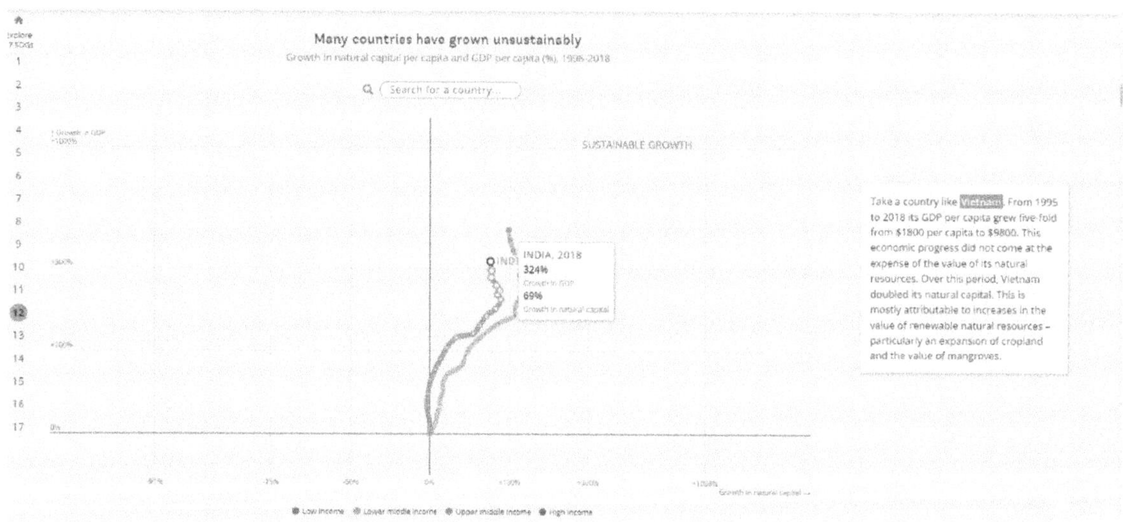

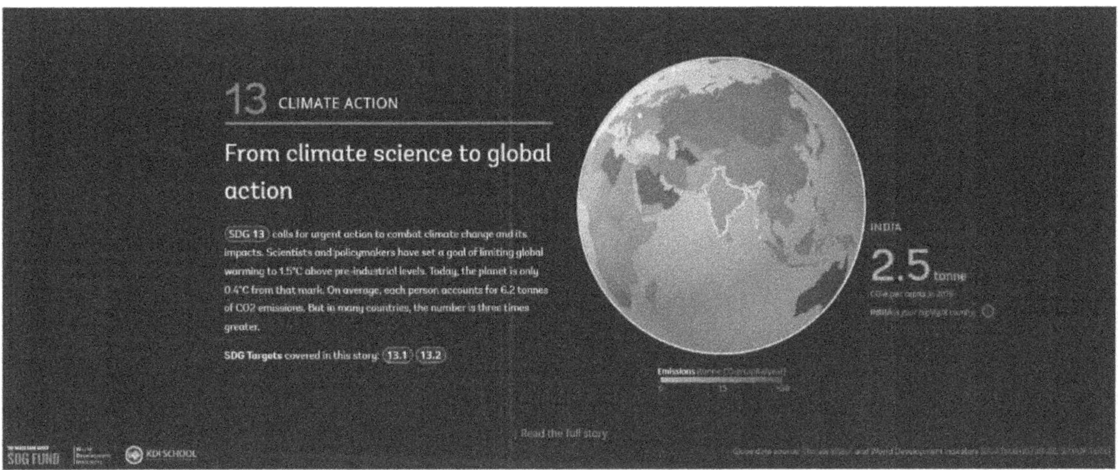

The past eight years (2015 to 2022) were the warmest on record.
The latest climate assessment report published by the Intergovernmental Panel on Climate Change (IPCC) confirms that the earth's atmosphere, ocean, and ecosystems are undergoing widespread and unprecedented changes.

Human activities are responsible for increases in greenhouse emissions, which lead to the warming of the atmosphere, ocean, and land.
Virtually all global warming over the last 200 years was caused by humans.

A number of greenhouse gases contribute to the warming.SDG target 13.2 Carbon dioxide (CO2) is the most important because once produced, it stays in the atmosphere for thousands of years. Other greenhouse gases include methane (CH_4), nitrous oxide, and fluorinated-gases. These do not remain in the atmosphere as long as CO_2, but have greater ability to absorb energy and cause warming. Global warming potential (GWP) is a metric used to estimate the ability of a gas to cause warming of the atmosphere relative to CO_2. For example, 1 ton of methane causes 27-30 times more warming than one 1 ton of carbon dioxide over a 100 year period.

Accounting for the global warming potential of the different gases, emissions can be compared and aggregated using CO_2 equivalent emissions. CO_2 equivalent (CO_2e) estimates the amount of carbon dioxide that results in the same warming for each gas.

In CO_2 equivalent terms, emissions from CO_2 contribute three-fourths of the total annual GHG emissions and methane contributes about one-sixth.

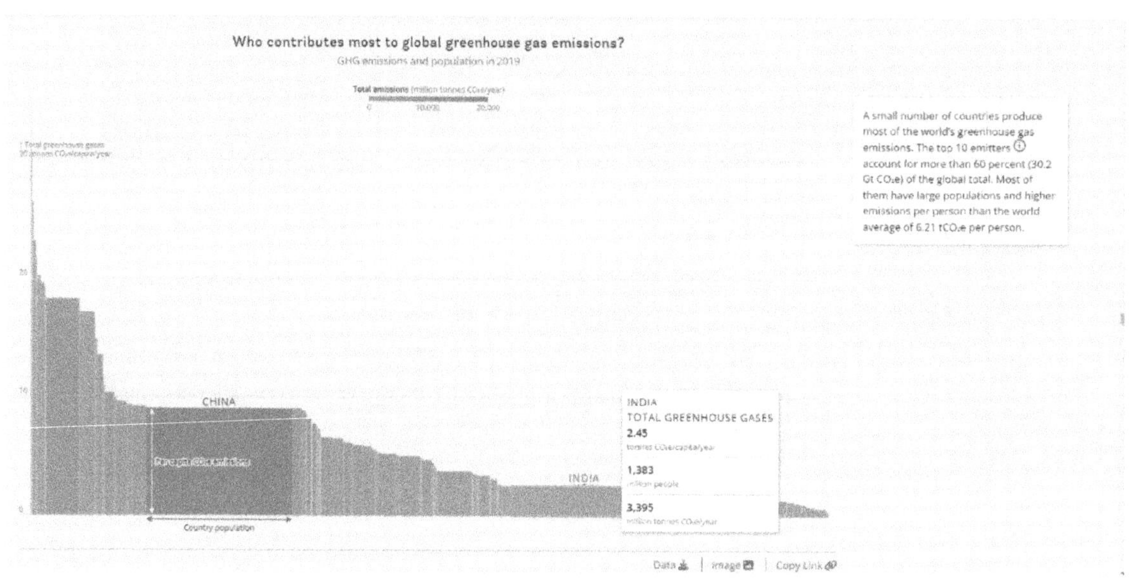

https://datatopics.worldbank.org/sdgatlas/goal-13-climate-action#c25s2

As of 2019, China topped the list, producing 26.4 percent of global greenhouse gas emissions (with 18 percent of global population), followed by the United States at 12.5 percent (with 4 percent of global population), India at 7.1 percent (with 18 percent of global population), and the European Union at 7.0 percent (with 6 percent of global population).

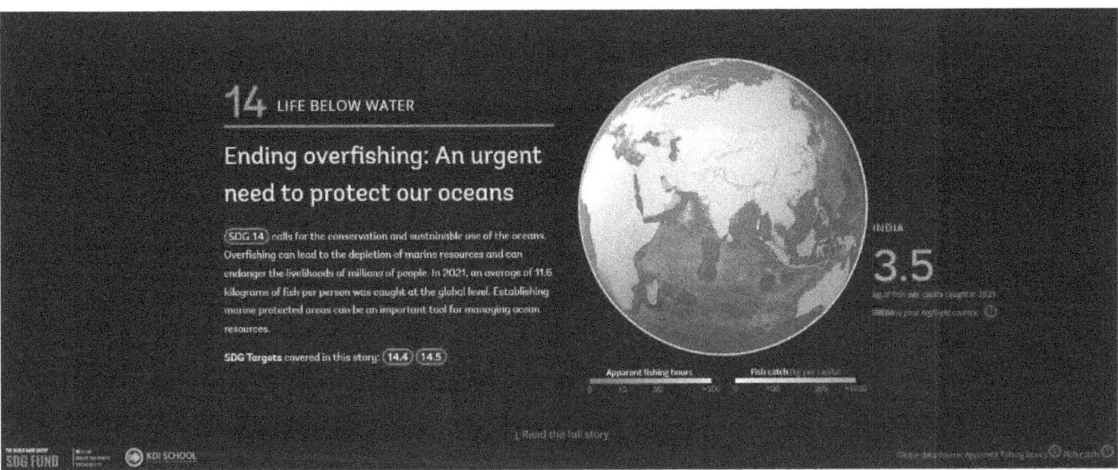

https://datatopics.worldbank.org/sdgatlas/goal-14-life-below-water#c3s4

SDG 14 aims to increase efforts to conserve and sustainably use the oceans. These efforts are measured and monitored through 10 interrelated targets. SDG target 14.4 is designed to regulate fishing activities and eliminate overfishing as well as illegal, unreported, unregulated, and destructive fishing. Overfishing occurs when too many fish are caught too quickly, without allowing time for the population to recover. This threatens the marine environment and the livelihoods of those who depend on it. This story also focuses on the implementation of SDG target 14.5 that focuses on the establishment of marine protected areas.

Global fish production has reached an all-time high
Fish production consists of capture production, which is defined as fish caught openly in the ocean or inland waters, and aquaculture production, which consists of farmed fish.

The **top 10 capture producers** in 2021 (China, Indonesia, Peru, Russia, United States, Vietnam, India, Japan, Norway, and Chile) represented 60 percent of the global total (excluding inland capture production).

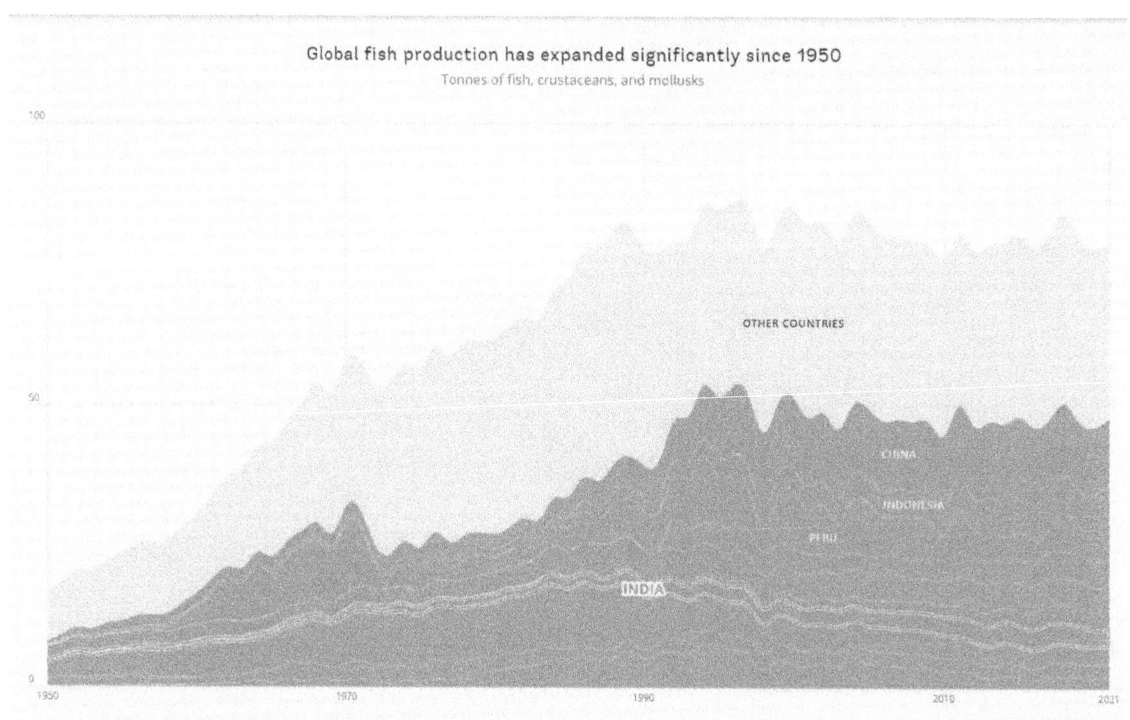

Capture production is increasing pressure on wild fish stocks. In addition, aquaculture contributes to this pressure because farmed fish are often fed with captured wild fish, like the Peruvian anchovy. It can take large quantities of small wild fish to feed the larger fish in farms.

Measuring and monitoring fish resources in the ocean is more challenging than monitoring resources on land. Illegal, unreported, and unregulated (IUU) fishing makes this even harder. It is estimated that one in every five fish caught comes from IUU fishing.

Source: FAO. 2023. Fishery and Aquaculture Statistics. Global production by production source 1950-2021 (FishStatJ). In: FAO Fisheries and Aquaculture Division. Rome. Updated 2023

Overfishing can also lead to the extinction of the large marine predators that feed on these stocks. In 2021, the IUCN released its assessment of around 1,200 species of sharks and rays concluding that the proportion of these that are threatened has increased from a quarter to a third between 2014 and 2021, most likely due to overfishing.

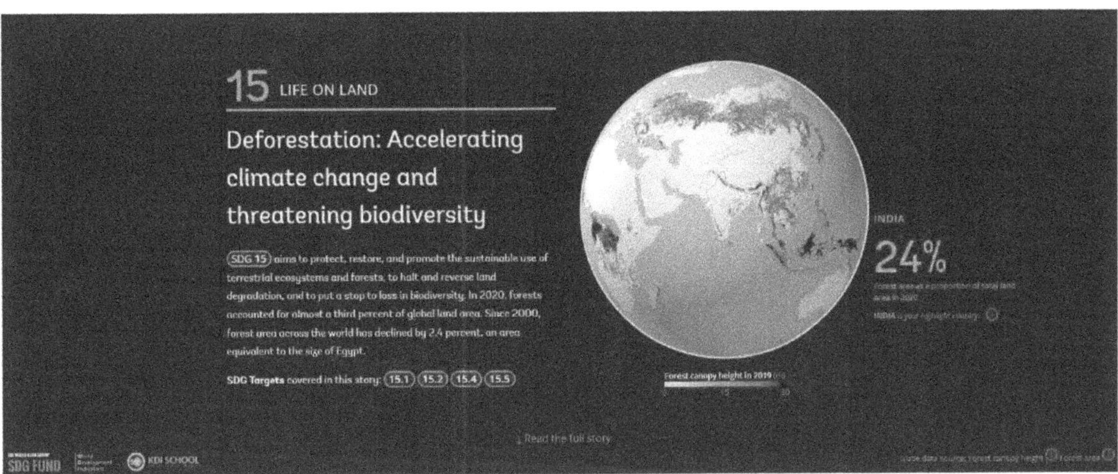

Covering almost one third of the Earth's land surface, forests offer a habitat to over 80 percent of all terrestrial species and are key to preserving biodiversity. SDG target 15.5 Forested watersheds and wetlands supply three quarters of all accessible freshwater in the world.

Worldwide an estimated 300 to 350 million people live in or close to forests and largely depend on them for their livelihoods; over a billion people rely on forests for employment, forest products, and contributions to livelihoods and income.

Many of those living in extreme poverty are highly dependent on forests for their livelihood. Forests play a key role in the mitigation of climate change, removing an estimated 16 billion tonnes of carbon dioxide (CO2) from the atmosphere annually, equalling a quarter of the annual CO2 released from burning fossil fuels.

Forest area is unequally distributed

Forest cover varies across the globe – some countries are predominantly forest while others have little or none. Over a quarter of global forest land is located in Russia, Brazil, Canada, and China. In 40 countries forest cover accounts for less than 10 percent of their total land area. The share of a country's land area that is forested is monitored under SDG target 15.1.

Forest cover is unequally distributed across the globe

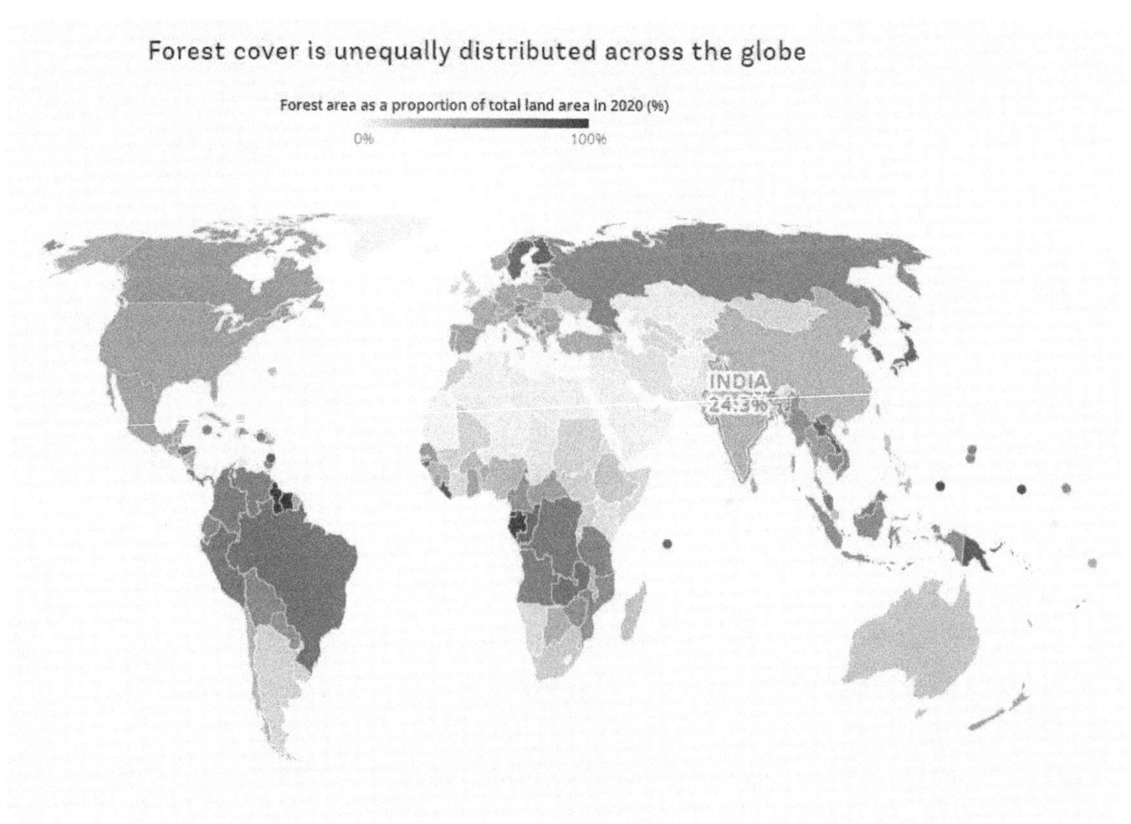

https://datatopics.worldbank.org/sdgatlas/goal-15-life-on-land#c3

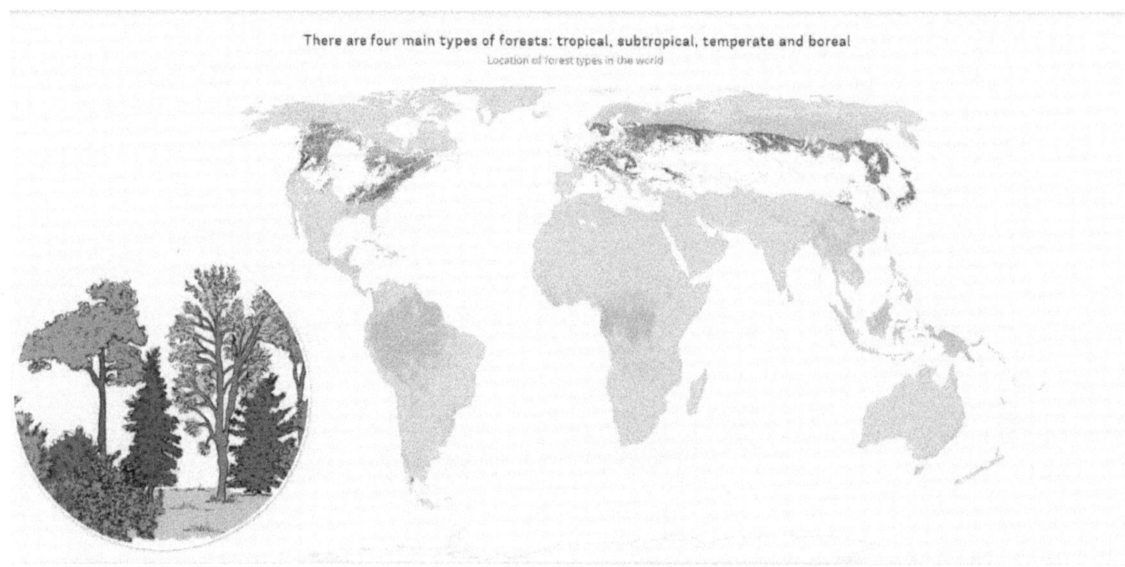

Deforestation and Degradation

Deforestation and forest degradation threaten the ability of forests to contribute to sustainable development

Forests are threatened by deforestation and degradation. The Food and Agriculture Organization (FAO) defines deforestation as the permanent transformation of forested areas to other land uses, such as agriculture or construction. Degraded forests have been damaged by human activities like logging or climatic and environmental events such as wildfires to the extent that their productive capacity is severely diminished. Degradation diminishes the quality of a forest' s vegetation and biodiversity, rather than reducing the overall forested area.

Net change in forest area between 2000 and 2020
-2.4%
WORLD

Losses and gains in forest land vary widely from country to country. Paraguay lost almost 30 percent of its forest between 2000 and 2020, mainly to convert land for cattle ranching. This contrasts with Vietnam, which implemented policies restricting logging and promoting reforestation, and increased forest area by 23 percent over the same period.

https://datatopics.worldbank.org/sdgatlas/goal-15-life-on-land#c11

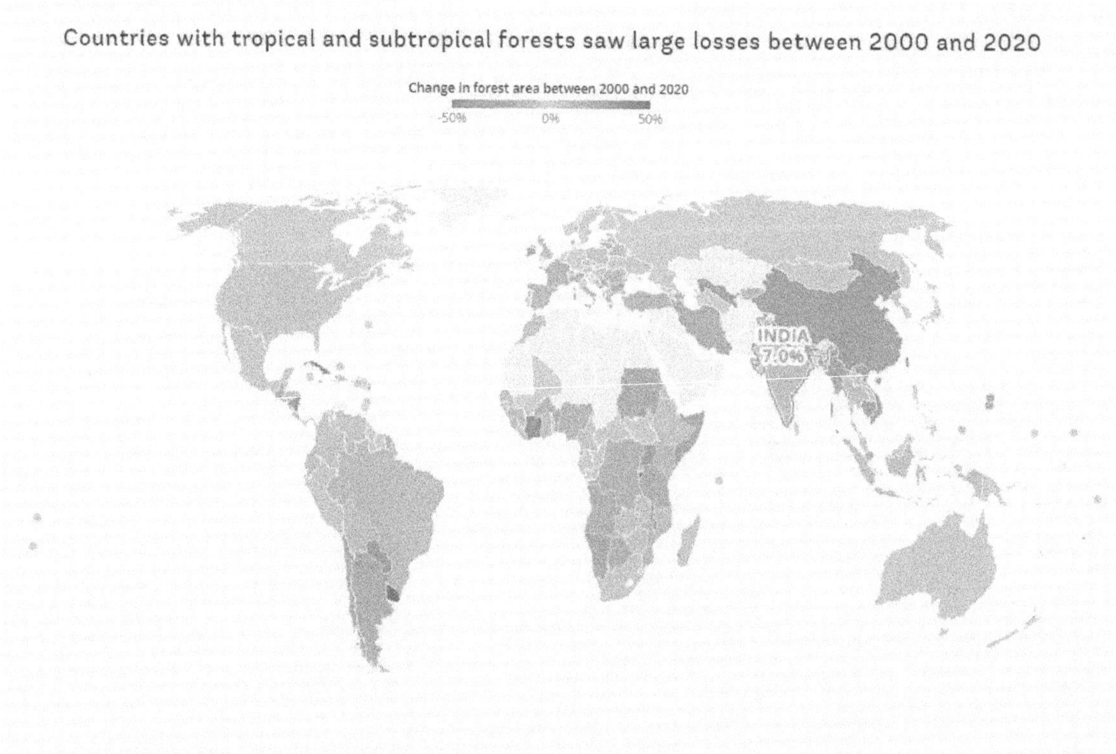

Total global tree cover loss between 2000 and 2021 was 11 percent.
The loss in 2021 alone was around 25 million hectares, an area comparable to the size of
Uganda, Ecuador or the United Kingdom.
The five main drivers of tree cover loss are commodity-driven agriculture, urbanization, shifting
agriculture, forestry, and wildfires.
The largest share of permanent tree cover loss occurred in the tropics, where the impact on
biodiversity and the climate is the heaviest.
The International Union for Conservation of Nature' s (IUCN) Red List of Threatened Species
seeks to categorize all species on the planet according to the extinction risk they face. Of nearly
150,000 species evaluated, 28 percent of these are classified as threatened with extinction.
The information in the Red List of Threatened Species can be used to guide conservation
efforts.

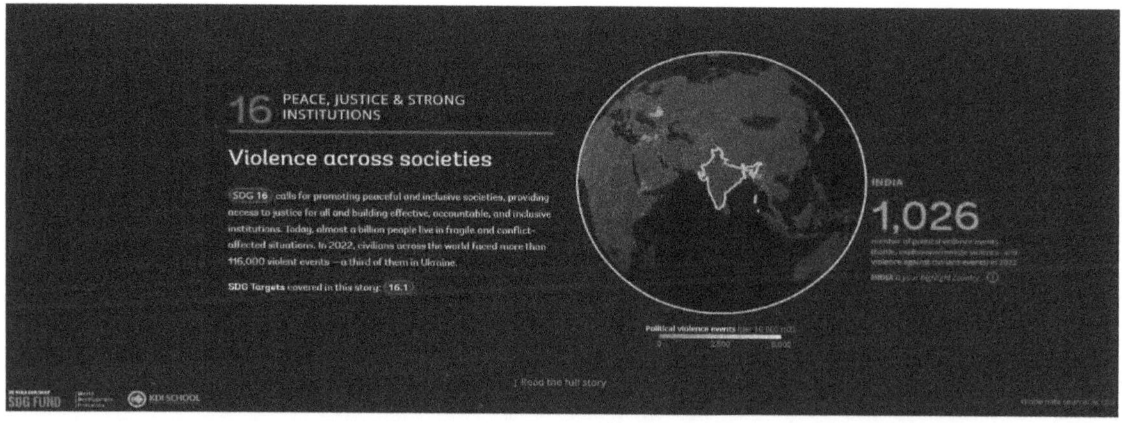

Homicide Rate

SDG 16 is about advancing just, peaceful, and inclusive societies and building effective, accountable, and inclusive institutions. The importance of safeguarding human life from violence has been recognized through SDG target 16.1 which calls for significantly reducing all forms of violence and related death rates everywhere. In addition to the lives lost, homicide and armed conflict erode trust among citizens, undermine development efforts, and result in lost economic output.

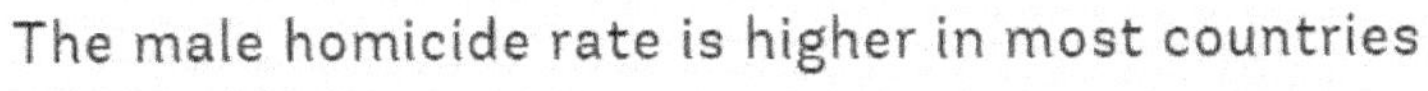

The male homicide rate is higher in most countries

Intentional homicides (per 100,000 people), by gender, 2020

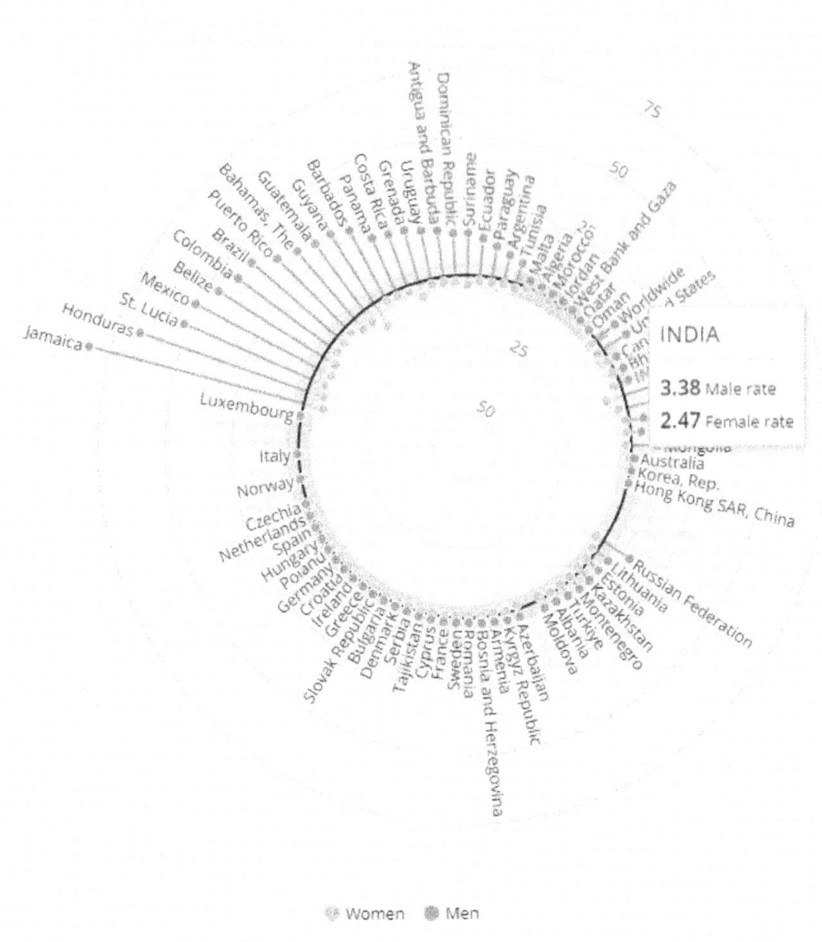

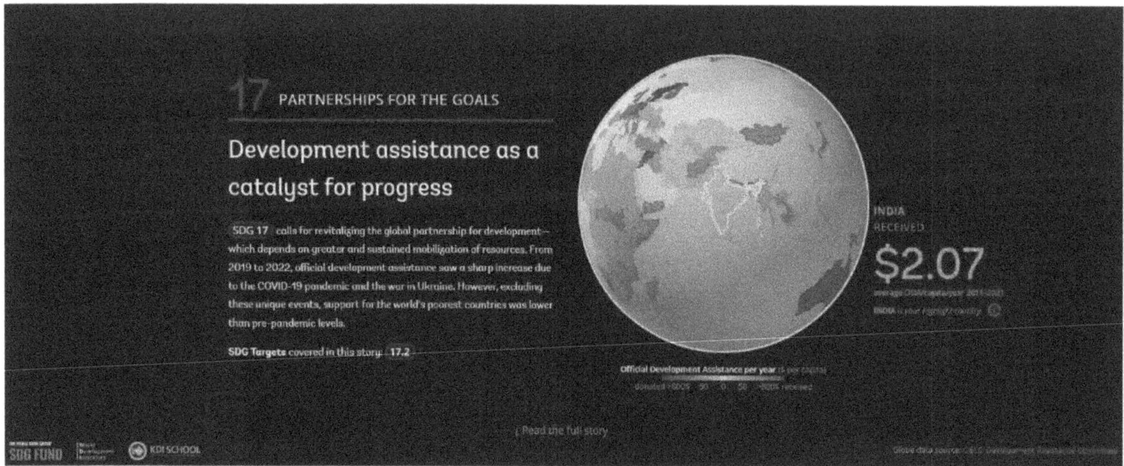

Progress toward the Sustainable Development Goals requires significant investment in programs, policies, human capital, and infrastructure. Official development assistance (ODA) from foreign governments supports the development of less wealthy countries. This aid typically flows to receiving governments through bilateral flows, or through non-governmental organizations or multilaterals, including the United Nations and the World Bank.

https://datatopics.worldbank.org/sdgatlas/goal-17-partnerships-for-the-goals#c15s0

Aid is at an all-time high, driven by the response to the war in Ukraine and the pandemic Funding from DAC countries has significantly increased in recent years for needs related to COVID-19 and Russia's invasion of Ukraine. Preliminary data for 2022 indicates that ODA reached a record $211.3 billion (in constant 2021 US dollars), an increase of nearly 28 percent since 2019 in real terms. This is one of the largest jumps observed over such a short time frame.

The surge in aid from 2019 to 2022 was driven by extraordinary spending related to the COVID-19 pandemic and the war in Ukraine. In 2021, nearly $22 billion or 11.7 percent of this funding was directed towards pandemic response, including vaccine donations. Numbers for 2020 and 2022 were about half that, but still a large part of overall ODA. In 2022, aid to Ukraine soared to $16.1 billion, from $918 million in 2021. The conflict in Ukraine also led to a tripling of spending on refugees arriving in donor countries from 2021 to 2022, totaling over $30 billion, nearly 15 percent of total ODA.
Without the pandemic assistance, in-donor-country refugee support, and direct aid to Ukraine, ODA would have declined 1.2 percent in real terms compared to pre-pandemic levels in 2019. In short: less aid has been allocated for activities not related to the pandemic and the war in Ukraine.

Absolute Spending by ODA

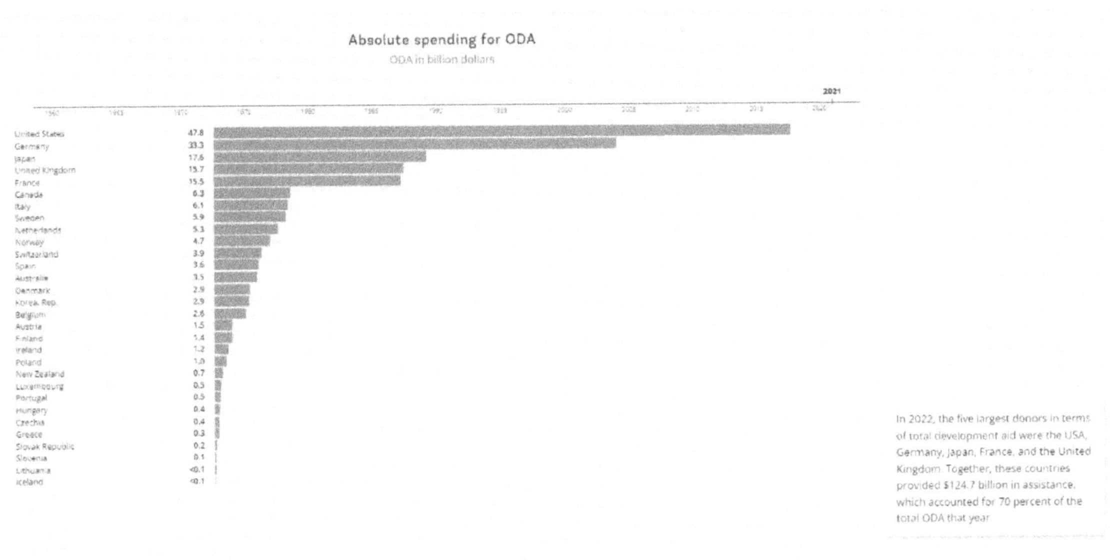

In 2022, the five largest donors in terms of total development aid were the USA, Germany, Japan, France, and the United Kingdom. Together, these countries provided $124.7 billion in assistance, which accounted for 70 percent of the total ODA that year.

Relative to the size of donor economies, aid remains short of targets.

Although official aid has reached a record high in absolute real terms, it remains modest as a percentage of donor countries' economies. The share of gross national income (GNI) dedicated to aid in DAC donor countries has hovered around 0.3 percent for the past 50 years, and reached a 40-year high of 0.36 percent in 2022.

This is barely above half the target for developed nations to allocate at least 0.7 percent of GNI for aid to less wealthy countries, as specified in SDG target 17.2. To meet this target collectively, donor countries would have to contribute an additional $200 billion in 2022, almost doubling current aid levels. The chart below illustrates the gap to the 0.7 percent target for DAC member countries in aggregate.

The gap could grow even larger in coming years if donor economies grow without substantially boosting aid, or if the pandemic and wartime support subsides.
Despite increasing in absolute numbers, ODA remains far from the target of 0.7% of GNI.

ODA target **2009: $294.18** billion

Actual ODA
$130.28 billion (**0.31% of GNI**)

Difference to ODA target
-$163.90 billion

Epilogue

Throughout this book, we've journeyed through the many ways in which indicators—GDP, inflation, literacy rates, environmental metrics, and more—attempt to capture the pulse of a nation. But as we've seen, these numbers, while powerful, are never the full story. Our challenge lies not just in collecting numbers, but in interpreting them with context, compassion, and clarity.

Behind every data point lies a lived reality: a child gaining access to school, a farmer facing rising input costs, a family navigating urban housing, a community adapting to climate stress. Indicators help us track change, but they also challenge us to ask deeper questions—about equity, sustainability, and the kind of development we truly value.

As we move forward, let us not just measure progress, but make sense of it. Let us use data not as a destination, but as a compass—one that guides policy, sparks dialogue, and keeps us anchored in the real stories of people and places.

www.ingramcontent.com/pod-product-compliance
Lightning Source LLC
Chambersburg PA
CBHW040209110726
48005CB00019B/2954